Wiley Global Finance is a market-leading provider of over 400 annual books, mobile applications, elearning products, workflow training tools, newsletters and websites for both professionals and consumers in institutional finance, trading, corporate accounting, exam preparation, investing, and performance management.

ADVANCED CHARTING TECHNIQUES FOR HIGH PROBABILITY TRADING

Founded in 1807, John Wiley & Sons is the oldest independent publishing company in the United States. With offices in North America, Europe, Australia and Asia, Wiley is globally committed to developing and marketing print and electronic products and services for our customers' professional and personal knowledge and understanding.

The Wiley Trading series features books by traders who have survived the market's ever changing temperament and have prospered—some by reinventing systems, others by getting back to basics. Whether a novice trader, professional or somewhere in-between, these books will provide the advice and strategies needed to prosper today and well into the future.

For a list of available titles, visit our Web site at www.WileyFinance.com.

ADVANCED CHARTING TECHNIQUES FOR HIGH PROBABILITY TRADING

The Most Accurate and Predictive
Charting Method Ever Created

Joseph Hooper
Aaron Zalewski
Ed Watanabe

WILEY

John Wiley & Sons, Inc.

Published by John Wiley & Sons, Inc., Hoboken, New Jersey.

Published simultaneously in Canada.

For general information on our other products and services or for technical support,
please contact our Customer Care Department within the United States at (800) 762-
2974, outside the United States at (317) 572-3993 or fax (317) 572-4002.

Wiley also publishes its books in a variety of electronic formats. Some content that
appears in print may not be available in electronic books. For more information about
Wiley products, visit our web site at www.wiley.com.

Library of Congress Cataloging-in-Publication Data:

Hooper, Joseph, 1943-
    Advanced charting techniques for high probability trading : the most accurate and pre-
dictive charting method ever created / Joseph Hooper, Aaron Zalewski, and Ed Watanabe.
        p. cm. — (Wiley trading series)
    Includes index.
    ISBN 978-1-118-43579-3 (cloth); ISBN 978-1-118-51597-6 (ebk);
ISBN 978-1-118-51598-3 (ebk); ISBN 978-1-118-51599-0 (ebk)
    1. Stocks—Charts, diagrams, etc.   2. Investment analysis.
I. Zalewski, Aaron, 1980-   II. Watanabe, Ed.   III. Title.
    HG4638.H66 2013
    332.63'2042—dc23
                                                    2012031973

Printed in the United States of America
10 9 8 7 6 5 4 3 2 1

To My Father, Frank Watanabe

I have stated in my advanced charting seminars that to be a successful trader, a person must practice discipline and perseverance and learn to follow rules. I dedicate this book to my father, Frank Watanabe, because he demonstrated those qualities to me as a young boy. My father came to America as a young man in his early twenties just before World War II broke out. Although he knew just a few English words, he demonstrated amazing bravery traveling to America in search of fulfilling his dream. He overcame extreme prejudice and adversity to become a very successful business-and family man. I am a product of that environment—an environment of discipline, perseverance, and following the rules of life.

—Ed Watanabe

CONTENTS

WARNING: Reading this book will change your life as a trader/investor.

Charting for me was a struggle for years as I tried to figure out how to interpret the many technical indicators that were available to use. Which ones should I use? Why is this one better than another one? How do I interpret what the lines mean? I attended many charting seminars, read many books, and still have a library of cassette tapes and videos on charting . . . I never found an answer to charting that satisfied me.

It wasn't until I attend my first Compound Stock Earnings seminar on trading covered calls that I again became very interested in charting. I had a renewed drive to master technical charting. Over the years with the advancement of charting software, many different charting programs became available to test. Many programs had features to change formulas and numerous charting criteria to make the indicators perform differently. This is was the birth of advanced charting.

I was determined to test, back-test, and change formulas. Finding the correct formulas took months of persistence and trial and error. This book is the fruit of my labor. It started with a drive to trade covered calls and make a consistent 3 to 4 percent per month and to improve those returns. Advanced charting has advanced even further with streaming data charts.

Why is advanced charting different than all other charting programs? The final version of 20 proprietary indicators have been redefined and reformulated after hundreds of tests. Why so many? Trading is all about probabilities. There are no absolutes and no guarantees. Every day is a new trading day that depends on the emotions of the marketplace. My indicators are designed to either agree or disagree with each other. There are many subtleties to learn to understand the various degrees of agreement. But we know that advanced charting works with thousands of experienced and first-time traders around the world who use it to enter and exit their trades with consistent profit. Do you want proof? Visit the Compound Stock Earnings Web site at www.compoundstockearnings.com.

There are hundreds of closed trades that show profits earned by using advanced charting. The learning curve is fast. Soon you will look at a stock chart and will be able to see confirmation, validation, and agreement that any given stock, exchange-traded fund, or index is about to cycle up or cycle down. Isn't that what trading is all about? Advanced charting will help you know when to enter and exit a trade and know when to protect profit.

I hope that you will enjoy this book. Advanced charting has changed the lives of many traders. I receive numerous e-mails from traders who have mastered it and are now able to generate cash every day that they trade. Many of these traders are now trading full time. You can do this too.

Enjoy.

Ed Watanabe

ADVANCED
CHARTING
TECHNIQUES
FOR HIGH
PROBABILITY TRADING

CHAPTER 1

Introduction to Advanced Charting

A dvanced Charting techniques have historically not been a part of the Compound Stock Earnings (CSE) method. Rather, the focus of the CSE method has been to understand simple bias in stock price direction and to act accordingly. To understand bias, we assess the stock's price cycle (the current movement of the stock price within a parallel range) and the position of the stock within that cycle.

When a stock is *high* in its current cycle, the bias is down. When a stock is *low* in the current cycle, the bias is up. To understand this bias, a simple straight-line, or open-high-low-close (OHLC) chart is used. This method of understanding simple bias has been applied, and proven successful, for years using the CSE covered call, LEAPS, and credit spread techniques.

The reason simple charting methods can be used successfully with the CSE covered calls, LEAPS, and credit spread techniques is that the techniques are based on probability. In a speculative stock or options trade, if the speculator picks the direction of the stock incorrectly, a loss on the position will be realized. In the CSE covered call methodology, if the assumed bias is incorrect, a loss is not generated. Rather, another management technique can be used to provide a solution. Therefore, when using the CSE covered call technique, an incorrect assumption of stock price direction does not result in the investor losing money; rather, it results in the investor needing to apply a management technique to rectify the situation. This is an important distinction between speculative trading and the CSE covered call/LEAPS techniques.

■ Why Use Charting?

Speculators have developed technical charting indicators due to the critical need to be correct in picking the direction of a stock—picking the stock price direction correctly is the only way speculators can profit from a trade. While that critical need is not present when using the CSE trading methods, increased accuracy in understanding bias leads to an increase in efficiency and returns when using the CSE techniques.

Technical chartists attempt to anticipate the direction of the next price tic and ultimately the direction of the cycle of the stock or index. Will the tic move up or down, and how long will it continue? Some call this speculation: attempting to judge the direction of the next move. Let there be no mistake. It *is* speculation, but it is based on probability. All trading is speculation because the movement of the price tic is an emotional event driven by fear and greed. It is impossible to know what global news event will happen to drive the markets up or down. But it is possible to know the *probabilities* of movement of the price tic by using Advanced Charting.

The reality is . . . all about probabilities. What are the probabilities that tomorrow the price tic will move in this direction? What are the probabilities that there is momentum in this cycle? What are the probabilities that this next cycle will be long, short, or flat?

Traders should be aware of these questions, even when trading conservatively following the CSE rules of traditional covered calls, LEAPS, or credit spreads. Charting might help traders to see into the future with a certain degree of accuracy to be proactive. Charting will improve traders' timing to enter and exit positions. But charting will not make us more profitable unless we can master it and understand precisely what the indicators are forecasting for us.

Advanced Charting's indicators have been modified, reformulated, and redefined with specific rules to follow as we analyze the 18 indicators as explained throughout this book. That is the difference between Advanced

Charting and all other charting programs. *Advanced Charting indicators are to be analyzed in a specific order of importance.*

Advanced Charting is simplified from most charting techniques so the learning curve is rapid. Traders can master Advanced Charting quickly. This book will help you master charting with amazing results.

Advanced Charting Techniques for High Probability Returns will increase your understanding of cycle direction and bias, which will lead to:

1. Higher percentage of new positions being exited on the delta effect, called out, or closed on the delta low bridge (DLB), or 10-cent rule. This results in a lower percentage of new positions requiring management.
2. Higher percentage of tethered slingshot (TSS) for income call sales resulting in profitable buybacks. This means a lower percentage of TSSs will require the use of a defensive technique, such as surrogate stock replacement (SSR).
3. Higher buyback returns on TSSs due to knowing when to stay in a profitable TSS. This results in higher returns on positions that are being managed.
4. Fewer positions that will have to be managed.

Improving efficiency in these four areas by using Advanced Charting techniques, can show a conservative increase of returns by 1 to 2 percent per month for covered calls, dramatically more for LEAPS, and substantial and consistent returns with credit spreads. As such, Advanced Charting techniques are *not* indispensable to the CSE covered call/LEAPS/credit spread investor, yet they result in increasing efficiency and returns. For those experienced with our CSE techniques, this knowledge is significant, as marginal increases in monthly returns lead to a dramatically higher compounding of an account over the long term.

This book outlines Advanced Charting techniques that can be successfully applied to the various CSE techniques. The rules and management techniques of CSE remain the same. What changes is *when* to execute those rules and management techniques on a particular position based on these advanced charting techniques.

Any technical charting is useless if we cannot master it. We must master the ability to interpret what the indicators are forecasting for us.

In this book, Advanced Charting indicators are reformulated with new definitions and a methodology of interpretation. These indicators are constantly being back-tested and tweaked to track the changes in cycles relative to market trends.

Attempting to apply default (standard) technical indicators and their definitions with Advanced Charting will complicate and hinder the ability to understand and use the method effectively.

Technical charting is a subjective and complicated field, but with Advanced Charting, we apply logic and practical common sense to the analytical process of understanding cycles and trends through chart pattern recognition. Once you have mastered Advanced Charting, you can trade anything with a higher degree of accuracy.

The momentum phase of the movement or cycle of a stock is the most profitable and important phase in the life cycle of a stock. Being able to identify this phase is not critical when trading covered calls, LEAPS, or credit spreads; however, being able to identify this phase will greatly improve profits.

Mastery of Advanced Charting eliminates position management of most trades once entered. This means that you have mastered the timing to enter, exit, and wait on the charts. You will be able to identify the four phases of a cycle: birth, momentum, exhaustion, and death.

■ Advanced Charting Techniques

Over 175 technical indicators have been created by traders, mathematicians, and chartists over the years. These technical indicators are never used alone but are applied in various combinations. The sole purpose of using technical indicators is to aid in determining the probabilities of the future direction of a given security.

If we tested and tried various combinations of technical indicators, we could create over 4 million various combinations. Trying to find the correct marriage between technical indicators, like trying to find the holy grail, has been an ongoing exercise of technical traders for years, and will continue for many decades to come. To arrive at the perfect technical indicator marriage, we must first define exactly what results we want to find with these indicators. The technical indicators presented in this book have been applied successfully to the CSE technique for years. Additionally, as with other CSE techniques, CSE will continue to test and back-test these indicators to fine-tune them to a perfect marriage over time.

Advanced Charting Features

Those familiar with the CSE Covered Call Toolbox know that it is constantly being improved with new features and new tools. And the Advanced Charting tool is itself an ongoing process of improvement and development.

It is important to note that the Advanced Charting system is designed to address one simple question: Is the V true or false? After reading this book, you will realize how simple this question is but how important it is to have an answer.

The chart of SDS in Figure 1.1 shows all the charting features turned on, including the trader's portfolio. The pivot point indicator for the RIMM chart in Figure 1.2 is not shown but has an on/off feature for either standard or modified candles that we review later. We review the functionality of all of the toolbox features later in this book.

FIGURE 1.1 SDS Charting Features

■ Validating the V

Those familiar with the CSE techniques are aware that position entry and management techniques are executed based on the formation of a bias V on the line chart. When a stock is in the upper 25 percent of the price cycle and makes a regular V on the chart, bias is up. When a stock is in the lower 25 percent of the price cycle and makes an inverted V on the line chart, bias is down. However, on occasions, the bias V proves to be false, and the stock price moves in the opposite direction of the one that was assumed. The entire focus of this book is to validate the V. By validating the V, traders dramatically reduce the incidence of the assumed bias being incorrect.

The goal of this book is to teach a simple, easy-to-learn, but highly accurate method of determining the future direction, momentum, and duration of a given stock and applying CSE management rules using these technical indicators.

■ Advanced Charting Upper and Lower Indicators

The RIMM chart in Figure 1.2 shows all Advanced Charting technical indicators. We will take this chart apart and explain throughout this book, step by step, what each indicator means and how each line works in relation to the other indicators. Chart reading is all about graphic similarities and pattern recognition.

FIGURE 1.2 RIMM Advanced Charting Tool Indicator

This book is easy to read and understand. Only a few complicated terms are used in explaining how these technical indicators work. It is not necessary to understand how these technical indicators are calculated or the formulas used to create them. It is important only to master how to interpret charting similarities of the indicators and learn to trust exactly what they are forecasting.

CHAPTER 2

Straight-Line Chart

The first indicator we establish is a simple, straight-line chart. Those familiar with Compound Stock Earnings (CSE) trading techniques are very accustomed to looking at charts and analyzing them. The function of the simple straight-line chart remains the same: We use it to identify the current cycle of the stock and the position in the current cycle and to see the regular and inverted bias V.

A line chart presents a graphic image (albeit limited) of where the price of a stock has traveled over a given time period. The closing prices are often seen as the most important ones to track. We follow closing prices to enter and exit positions and to apply all CSE management rules. All line charts will produce Vs. The challenge for any trader tracking a line chart is validating the V. All of the technical indicators we study have been applied, tested, and back-tested to validate the V. We therefore will be able to determine whether a V is true or false.

Validating the V is the single most important skill that traders must learn. Mastery of this skill will improve your timing when entering new positions and tethered slingshots (TSSs). It will also increase your patience and allow you to gain added confidence with your decisions. Your ability to master validating the V is based solely on your ability to understand several very important and simple technical indicators.

The chart in Figure 2.1 shows the simple line chart as it travels, creating Vs, or changes, in closing prices. Trading covered calls is very forgiving. It is not necessary to know the *exact* place or time to enter a new position, just a general area of when to enter it. Obviously the more control that we have over patience and timing, the more profitable our trades will be. Ideally we want to BTO (buy to open) new positions at point 1 and STC (sell to close) at point 2 (see Figure 2.1). This position is a perfect example of a 10-cent rule trailing stop.

FIGURE 2.1   RRBG—The Line Chart

1. Point 1 is an ideal V to enter a new position.
2. The inverted Vs shown on this chart between point 1 and point 2 were false, giving us confidence to stay in the position for a large return on the 10-cent rule.

And how do we know that?

3. Point 3 is an ideal place to execute a TSS, whereas the inverted Vs immediately preceding it are false.

The daily movement of the tic up or down is an emotional event. It is the result of news or events around the world related to fear, greed, and other emotions.

The interpretation of these events has a direct effect on the market. The daily global premarket reports cause the major markets in America to move either up or down.

Technical charting indicators are the only way to track this movement to create a visual graphic so traders can determine the probability of cycle direction.

■ Straight-Line Charting/ Parallel Channels

Straight-line charts, which are made up of support and resistance lines, are drawn to determine the direction of a trend with the expectation that a trend line will define cycles (see Figure 2.2). The challenge for all traders is to determine the approximate lower 25 percent or the upper

DOWN TREND

FIGURE 2.2   DJI—Parallel Channels

FIGURE 2.3   DJI—Parallel Channel Challenge

75 percent of the cycle. This technique can be accurate if the trader can identify the trend line early in its path, and if the trend will remain in that path.

The challenge, however, is to identify a cycle that is about to bend or change the trend line, as in mid-March. The result is a cycle where the tic breaks through resistance undetected by straight-line charting (see Figure 2.3). Advanced Charting addresses this problem by identifying the change in cycle direction *before* it happens.

CHAPTER 3

Direction of a Trend

O ne of the basics of understanding any technical charting program is to understand cycles and trends. It is critical to understand how repeating cycles define, direct, and bend a trend line. A series of repeating upward-moving cycles, where the high of the cycle is higher than the previous cycle, ultimately defines a trend line. The trend line will begin to angle upward.

When the cycles begin to change where the higher highs are now lower than the previous high and the lower lows are now lower than the previous low, the trend line will begin to change its direction. The URBN chart shown in Figure 3.1 illustrates how repeating cycles define a trend line.

The two-year view of the DIA chart in Figure 3.2 shows how repeating cycles will change the trend of the stock. It is important to note that within each of the cycles of this two-year chart, there are numerous cycles and trends occurring. Advanced Charting is all about identifying these cycles relative to their trends.

FIGURE 3.1 URBN—Cycles and Trends

FIGURE 3.2 DIA—Cycles and Trends

■ Four Phases of a Cycle

Advanced Charting allows traders to look into the future with a higher degree of probability to determine the four phases of a cycle, which are:

1. Birth phase
2. Momentum phase
3. Exhaustion phase
4. Death phase

Every cycle will move through these four phases. However, the time duration of the phases distinguishes one cycle from another. Some cycles are short and others are long. A long up cycle may be followed by a short down cycle and then another long up cycle. The time duration of a cycle is the strength or weakness of the four phases The length of a cycle indicates how strong the phases are.

Upward Cycles

There are four upward cycles:

1. **Upward-cycle birth phase.** An upward-cycle birth phase is the lowest point of the cycle. Advanced charting and the interpretation of the lower indicators allow traders to determine the probabilities that this event is in fact occurring. If the birth phase is real, it will be followed by the momentum phase. Note, that not all "low" points of a cycle will be the birth phase. This fact is studied in more detail in Chapter 4.

2. **Upward-cycle momentum phase.** An upward momentum phase is the most important phase to identify. This is the sweet spot of the cycle. The momentum phase is when a stock tic advances rapidly upward. This phase can last for days, weeks, or even months. Those familiar with the CSE trading methodologies will immediately see the rewarding benefits of identifying this phase.

3. **Upward-cycle exhaustion phase.** The exhaustion phase is also an important phase to identify. This phase is also known as the greed factor. After we have entered the momentum phase and have been rewarded with a good profit, we must identify signs of the exhaustion phase. This is the first sign that a new down cycle may be about

to start. If it is ignored or not identified, the price tic may turn down rapidly and potentially large profits are given back and possibly lost. This book studies the signs of exhaustion in detail in Chapter 4.

4. **Upward-cycle death phase.** The death phase is the end of a cycle just before a new cycle starts. This phase may be very short with the new birth phase starting quickly. Or it may take several days for a new cycle to begin. Advanced charting indicators allow traders to develop patience and learn to recognize signs that mean: Do not trade, but wait for confirmation and validation that a new cycle is about to begin.

Downward Cycles

The four downward cycles are:

1. **Downward-cycle birth phase.** A downward-cycle birth phase is the highest point of the cycle. Advanced charting and the interpretation of the lower indicators allow traders to determine the probabilities that this event is in fact occurring. If the birth phase is real, it will be followed by the momentum phase. Note that not all "high" points of a cycle will be the birth phase. We discuss this topic in more detail in later chapters.

2. **Downward-cycle momentum phase.** A downward momentum phase is an equally important phase to identify. This is the sweet spot of the cycle for a profitable tethered slingshot (TSS). The momentum phase is when a stock tic advances rapidly downward. This phase can last for days, weeks, or even months. It is important to note that stocks generally drop faster than they rise. Those familiar with the CSE trading methodologies immediately see the benefits of identifying this phase.

3. **Downward-cycle exhaustion phase.** The downward exhaustion phase is also an important phase to identify. This phase is also known as the greed factor. After we have entered the TSS momentum phase and have been rewarded with a good profit, we must identify signs of the exhaustion phase. This is the first sign that a new upward cycle may be about to start. If it is ignored or not identified, the price tic may turn up rapidly. Not identifying this phase can cause traders to get behind on the TSS. This means the cycle is now moving upward and the short option is getting expensive for an adjustment buyback. Therefore,

potentially large TSS profits are given back and possibly lost. We study the signs of exhaustion in detail in Chapter 4.

4. **Downward-cycle death phase.** The downward death phase is the end of a cycle just before a new cycle starts. This phase may be very short with the new birth phase starting quickly. Or it may take several days for a new cycle to begin. Advanced charting indicators allow traders to develop patience and learn to recognize signs that mean: Do not trade, but wait for confirmation and validation that a new cycle is about to begin.

Understanding the four phases of a cycle and how Advanced Charting indicators allow traders to see the phase coming is paramount to the mastery of the technique.

The chart of DIA in Figure 3.3 shows the four phases of a cycle.

1. Birth phase—light green arrow
2. Momentum phase —dark green arrow
3. Exhaustion phase—lime green arrow
4. Death phase—red arrow

FIGURE 3.3 DIA Chart—Four Phases of a Cycle

It is important to note that phases can change rapidly from one phase to another. Phases can be very short or very long, but all cycles go through all four phases.

We have now explained how repeating cycles will define trends for both upward and downward moving stocks. However, the challenge with any charting program is to determine which indicators will confirm and validate these four important phases with consistency and accuracy. Advanced charting has formulated technical indicators specifically to address this challenge.

There are no absolutes or guarantees with any technical charting tools. Trading is all about probabilities. Advanced charting uses 18 technical indicators to determine the probability that the cycle will move in a specific direction.

Why 18 indicators? The Advanced Charting tool in the CSE toolbox has two charts: Window 1—Chart 1 (on the upper left) and Window 2—Chart 2 (on the upper right). Under each chart there are four lower indicators.

The two charts and their technical indicators were reformulated from traditional charting techniques to find the answer to one question: Is the V of the tic true or false? The definitions of these indicators have been reworked within a new methodology to interpret what the indicators are confirming and validating (Chapters 1 to 7 show Window 1—Chart 1 types; see Chapter 8 for more on Chart 2 types.).

■ Moving Averages Defined

A large part of our technical analysis is centered on moving averages (MAs). In this section we define what a moving average is and then discuss the moving averages used with the CSE techniques.

A moving average is an indicator frequently used in technical analysis showing the average value of a stock price over a set period of time. Moving averages are generally used to measure momentum and define areas of possible support and resistance.

Moving averages are used to emphasize the direction of a cycle and to smooth out price and volume fluctuations, or noise, that can confuse chart interpretation. Typically, upward momentum is confirmed when a short-term average crosses above a longer-term average. Downward momentum is confirmed when a short-term average crosses below a long-term average. We study momentum in more detail in Chapter 4.

Each new day's (or week's or month's) numbers are added to the average at the front and the oldest numbers are dropped at the end; thus, the average "moves" forward over time. In general, the shorter the time frame used, the more volatile the prices will appear. For example, 25-day MA lines tend to move up and down more than the M3 (blue) MA line. M3 (blue) MA lines will move more than the 100-day MA.

Key Points to Moving Averages

- MAs move more slowly than the price of the stock. They also are called lagging indicators.

- The current stock price has very little impact on moving averages because a moving average is an average of a certain body of data.

- Therefore, MAs are "gentle" indicators.

- They are very easy to use.

- If the latest price of the stock is above the MA, the stock will trade at a higher level than its average over the last X days, and vice versa.

We study the combination of five different moving averages developed exclusively for, and applied directly to, the CSE techniques.

■ Moving Average 1: Lead MA1 (White) M1

The lead MA (white) is the most important Moving Average that we will study. It is the most important indicator, and we must gain trust in reading the direction of the lead MA (white): up, down, or flat. It is called the lead dog, similar to the lead dog of a sled race (see Figure 3.4). Where the lead dog goes, so goes the sled. Where the lead MA (white) goes, so goes the other MAs. We explain the real significance of this analogy as we look at all moving averages together. The lead MA is called "M1."

Remember this visual: The lead MA (white), M1, is the lead dog. Where M1 (white) goes, the other MAs follow. Why? M1 (white) is an exponential moving average. Remember that what forms the M1 (white) line is higher highs and higher lows or lower highs and lower lows. In order for M1 (white) to be dramatically up or down, there must be dramatically higher or lower highs and lows. This is graphically illustrated by M1 (white). It is important to grasp this concept and learn to trust it.

FIGURE 3.4   Lead Dog

Just as the sled racer must have complete trust in the lead dog, traders must gain the same confidence in reading the lead MA (white) M1 on our charts. In Chapter 4 we explain how to read M1 (white) and validate it with other indicators.

The chart in Figure 3.5 is an example of M1 (white) and its relationship to the stock price. Look for M1 (white) in a dramatically up or down position.

M1 (white) is represented by the wide white line on the chart. This indicator plots the average price of a security over a short period, with more value being assigned to the most recent data. We use a bold white line because this line is the most important indicator to watch. It is bold so it is easy to see.

M1 (white) is the most important indicator, as it combines optimally with our other technical indicators to provide an accurate picture of bias. We must learn to trust M1.

FIGURE 3.5 —DY—M1

Notice that M1 (white) moves up in an upward angle because the stock is closing with higher highs and higher lows. Another important characteristic of this MA is that M1 (white) is weighted more heavily to the most recent day's data. M1 (white) also moves down in a downward angle because the stock is closing with lower highs and lower lows. M1 (white) moves to a horizontal or flat line because the highs and lows are averaging out or are converging.

As M1 (white) is a weighted average toward the most recent data, it is a highly valuable moving average in understanding the direction of the daily movement of the price tic. When the M1 (white) flattens out and changes direction, the stock's cycle may be changing direction.

The steepness of the angle, upward or downward, tells us the strength and momentum of the cycle. M1 (white) used in conjunction with other MAs and other technical indicators gives us a simple but yet very accurate method of trading the cycle.

Chart of DY—M1 (White)

On the chart of DY in Figure 3.6, note the higher highs and higher lows of M1 (white) as the stock cycles upward. Also note the lower highs and lower lows of M1 (white) as the stock cycles lower. This is very important to identify the "cycle rhythm" that all stocks create as the stock cycles up and down. Cycle rhythm is reviewed in more detail in Chapter 3.

On the chart of DY, note the relationship of the price movement (tic) to M1 for both the uptrending and downtrending cycle. M1 is formulated to interpret the movement the price tic as it moves up and down. A series of higher highs and higher lows causes M1 to turn and bend upward. The day-to-day movement of the price tic, or noise, is removed, and M1 proceeds to move gently upward.

The downward move of the price is a series of lower highs and lower lows of the price tic. This causes M1 to turn and bend downward. The day-to-day movement of the price tic, or noise, is removed, and M1 proceeds to move gently downward.

FIGURE 3.6   Chart of DY—M1

Chart of FSS—M1 (White)

On the chart of FSS in Figure 3.7, note the relationship of the price movement to M1 and the numerous downtrending cycles. Remember that the
tic price of the stock always leads M1 and is out in front of the M1. Why?
As in the case of FSS in August, the dramatic downward angle of M1 is the
result of daily lower highs and lower lows of the tic. The price tic is leading out in front of M1, and M1 is headed down dramatically.

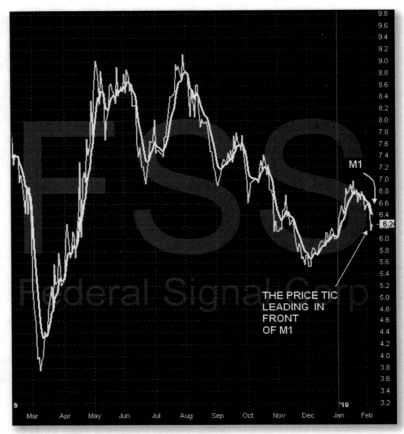

FIGURE 3.7 Chart of FSS—M1

A very important characteristic of M1 to note is that it becomes support for dramatically upward-trending stocks and resistance for dramatically downward-trending stocks. The chart in Figure 3.7 shows that when the stock price is moving up, M1 becomes support. When the stock is moving down, M1 becomes resistance. We study this in greater detail when we review the relationship of the upper Bollinger band to M1 and how the price tic moves between these two indicators in chapter 5. This is an extremely important element of a successful 10-cent rule or TSS. In sharply upward- or downward-moving cycles, M1 becomes support or resistance for the stock.

Chart of AA—M1 (White)

Note the stock price of AA shown in Figure 3.8 as it moves up and bounces off of M1. We must train our eyes to see this important relationship of the upward angle of M1 and the stock price. The stock price cannot and will not do anything but bounce off of M1 as it moves upward. We note this at several places on this chart.

In sharply upward- or downward-moving cycles, M1 becomes support or resistance for the stock.

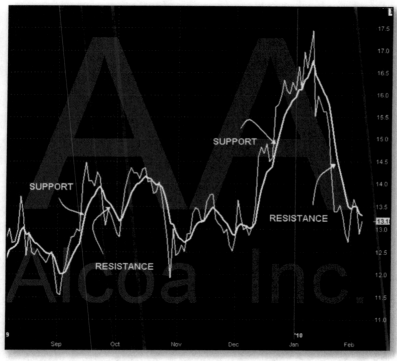

FIGURE 3.8 Chart of AA—M1

Chart of AMAT—M1 (White)

On chart of AMAT shown in Figure 3.9, try to identify the dramatic upward-moving M1 and the stock price (yellow line) as it bounces off of M1. It should be obvious that for downward-moving stocks, the same principles apply. Note the downward-moving M1 and the stock price as it also bounces off of M1. Go back to the previous chart examples and look for similar patterns with the stock price as it bounces off the lead MA (white) M1.

In sharply upward- or downward-moving cycles, M1 becomes support or resistance for the stock.

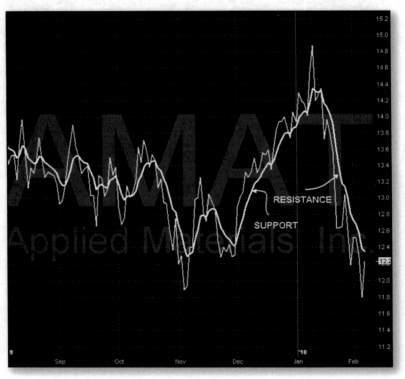

FIGURE 3.9   Chart of AMAT—M1 (White)

▇ Moving Average 2: M2 (Green)

M2 (green) is the second moving average indicator that we use and is represented by the green line on the chart in Figure 3.10. This indicator plots the average price of a security over a longer period of time with all data given equal weight. We want this moving average to be smooth and gentle. We study the relationship of M1 (white) and M2 (green) as M2 (green) validates the momentum of M1 and as M1 (white) and M2 (green) cross each other at various angles. We focus on the importance of the severity of the angle and what it indicates.

Moving averages flatten out large price fluctuations. Therefore, trends are easier to identify. When moving averages are used in combination,

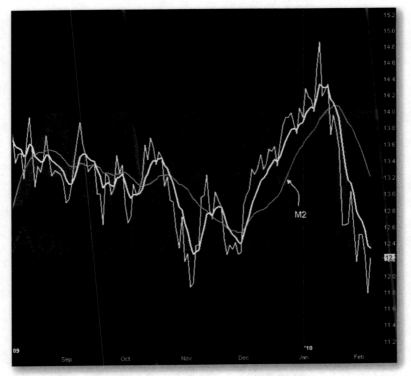

FIGURE 3.10 Chart of AMAT—M2 (Green)

the relationship identifies possible changes in cycle direction, momentum, and duration of a given price move. M2 (green) used with M1 (white) is an important indicator to watch as M1 (white) arches up to cross M2 (green) or arches down to cross back over M2 (green). Another important indicator is M1 (white) and M2 (green) as they move parallel to each other in either a dramatically up cycle or a dramatically down cycle. This is another validation of a strong upward or downward movement of the stock price.

Chart of AMAT—M1 (White) and M2 (Green)

In the chart example of AMAT in Figure 3.11, note the relationship of M1 (white) above M2 (green) and M1 (white) below M2 (green). When M1 (white) is moving above M2 (green), the stock is generally in an upward cycle. When M1 (white) is moving below M2 (green), the stock is

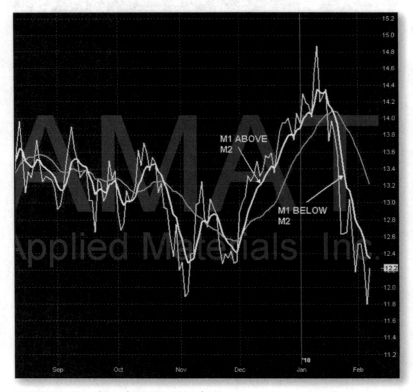

FIGURE 3.11   Chart of AMAT—M1 and M2

generally in a downward cycle. It is also important to note the angle of M2 (green) relative to M1 (white).

If M2 (green) is tracking the angle of M1 (white), this indicates the beginning of a strong cycle. This is agreement, confirmation, and validation of the direction of the cycle as M2 follows M1.

Chart of AA—M1 (White) and M2 (Green)

On the chart of AA in Figure 3.12, note the relationship of the price movement to M1 (white) and M2 (green). Watching the position of M1 (white) relative to M2 (green) gives us the cycle direction. When M1 (white) is above M2 (green), the cycle is up; when M2 (white) is below M2 (green), the cycle is down.

When M1 (white) turns up and crosses M2 (green) from the bottom, we see the establishment of an upward cycle in the stock price. When

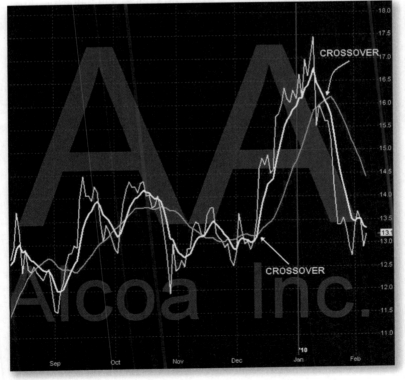

FIGURE 3.12   Chart of AA—M1 and M2 Crossover

M1 (white) turns down and crosses M2 (green) from the top, we see the establishment of a downward cycle in the stock price.

■ Moving Average 3: M3 (Blue)

The M3 (blue) is represented by the blue line on the chart in Figure 3.13. This indicator plots the average price of a security over a longer period, longer than both M1 (white) and M2 (green), with all data given equal weight.

M3 (blue) is similar to M2 (green) and is used only to validate and confirm the strength and momentum of the cycle. All moving averages are lagging indicators. M3 (blue) is lagging way behind but is used to confirm and validate that a strong price move is occurring. A strong price move is confirmed when all three moving averages are stacked and moving in the same direction.

If the duration of this move is strong, M3 (blue) will follow the direction of M2 (green). For a stacked upward-trending stock, the MAs will be in this order:

- M1 (white) will be above M2 (green) and M3 (blue).

- M2 (green) will be above M3 (blue).

- The moment M2 crosses M3, it is technically stacked. However, at this early stage, M1 (white) and M2 (green) may not be moving in the same direction.

- When M3 (blue) turns to follow M2, this confirms and validates momentum.

- Note: M3 is a lagging indicator and may not be moving in the same direction as M2, but momentum could be building. We study this more in detail when we review the lower indicators in Chapter 7.

When M1 (white), M2 (green), and M3 (blue) are positioned in this order, they are stacked, and this indicates a strong price movement. This is the momentum phase.

Chart of DELL—M1 (White), M2 (Green), M3 (Blue) Stacked Up

Look at the DELL chart in March (Figure 3.13). This chart is typical for a strong upward cycle with M1 (white) crossing over M2 (green) and then crossing M3 (blue). M2 (green) then crosses over M3 (blue), and all moving averages are now stacked up. M1 (white) is above M2 (green), then M2 (green) and M3 (blue) are both under M1 in that order. This indicates an uptrending cycle with very strong momentum.

Identifying these cycles allows for very large returns on KADD and the 10-cent rule transactions. It allows for great certainty of exiting the position versus going into management. We discuss this in depth later in Chapter 7. We can time the perfect entrance of a new position by first identifying the birth of a new cycle followed by the beginning of the momentum phase. Understanding the lower indicators, which we review later in Chapter 7, is the key to knowing when to pull the trigger.

FIGURE 3.13 Chart of DELL—M1, M2, and M3 Stacked Up

Chart of M1 (White), M2 (Green), M3 (Blue) Stacked Down

On the DELL chart in mid-August (Figure 3.14), note the crossover of M1 (white) over M2 (green) and then crossing over M3 (blue). When M1 (white) crosses M2 (green) and M2 (green) crosses M3 (blue), this indicates a change in momentum—in this case, a strong downward cycle began. When M3 (blue) begins to follow M2 (green) (late August), this validates strong momentum and the duration of this cycle direction. At this point, all three MAs are stacked down. This indicates a downward-trending cycle with very strong momentum.

Identifying the stacked-down formation and the false Vs, as the stock price bounces off of M1 (white), allows us to achieve incredible returns using the TSS. Timing the perfect entry for a TSS is possible by identifying the end of momentum, the beginning of exhaustion, and the birth of a new downward cycle. Understanding the lower indicators, which we review later in Chapter 7, is the key to knowing when to pull the trigger.

FIGURE 3.14 Chart of DELL—M1, M2, M3 Stacked Down

CHAPTER 4

Moving Average Crossovers

Now that we understand the movement of the three key moving averages, the lead moving average (MA) M1 (white), M2 (green), and M3 (blue), it is time to discuss moving average crossovers in depth and why MA crossovers are extremely important to Advanced Charting. As a stock or index moves up, down, or flat in its cycle, it moves through four phases. We reviewed this briefly on the chart in Figure 3.3 and study this topic in detail in this chapter. All cycles have four phases:

1. Birth
2. Momentum
3. Exhaustion
4. Death

■ M1 (White) Crossing M2 (Green)

As mentioned earlier, these four phases indicate the stock is about to change direction. To determine this, we look at the lead dog—M1 (white). When a stock is rising, we know that eventually M1 (white) will flatten out and go horizontal, turn over, point down, and then cross over M2 (green).

Crossovers of M1 (white) to M2 (green) give us a very good early indication of a possible change in cycle direction. This is a very important relationship to understand. When we are tracking the stock in real time, we should be watching for M1 (white) to turn direction and head toward M2 (green). This is an early indication of a possible change in cycle direction. Watching for this change allows us to pick up a move from a declining cycle to a rising cycle, or vice versa, before there is a break to the top or bottom of the cycle (as identified by a parallel channel).

Look at the chart in Figure 4.1 in mid-February. See how M1 (white) turns up sharply and crosses over M2 (green). This crossover actually happens within the declining cycle. The MAs are telling us that the cycle direction is about to change. More important, they are telling us before the stock breaks to the top of the declining cycle.

FIGURE 4.1 Chart of DE—M1, M2 Crossover

Look at the same chart in mid-March. As the stock reaches the overbought area of its cycle, M1 (white) flattens out or starts to move horizontally.

If the cycle has entered into the exhaustion phase, M1 (white) will continue to arch over. See M1 (white) as it turns down sharply and starts heading toward M2 (green). For the first time since early March, it is actually pointing down. Again, this movement provides us with a very early indication that the cycle direction may be about to change from up to down. When M1 (white) actually crosses M2 (green), we may have a change in cycle direction. Again, the MAs are picking up a potential change in cycle direction before the stock breaks to the bottom of the next rising cycle.

This is an important point and an enhancement over traditional channel lines of line charts.

■ M1 (White) Crossing M2 (Green) and Then Crossing M3 (Blue)

In the previous example, we saw an early indication of a change in cycle direction by watching M1 (white) cross M2 (green). We are now going to extend this an extra step and look at M1 (white) continuing on to cross M3 (blue).

M2 (green) continues and crosses M3, and the MAs are now all stacked in one direction.

Look at the chart in Figure 4.2. In mid-June, we see the moving averages crossing over and becoming stacked up. We now know this is a period of upward momentum. In early August, we see M1 (white) cross M2 (green). We now know that this is a strong indication that the cycle has exhausted itself. We then see M1 (white) continue to move downward and M2 (green) cross M3 (blue). Now we have all MAs stacked down, indicating strong downward momentum.

■ 12 Key Points of M1, M2, and M3 Crossovers

The chart of BMY (Figure 4.3) shows various moving average crossovers. What do these crossovers indicate, and what are we watching for? Let's highlight the crossovers at each point and discuss their meaning (see Figures 4.4 through 4.15). The four phases of a cycle—birth, momentum, exhaustion, and death—are all illustrated in these examples.

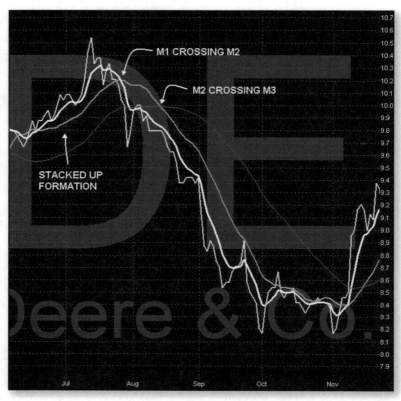

FIGURE 4.2   Chart of DE—M1, M2, M3 Crossover

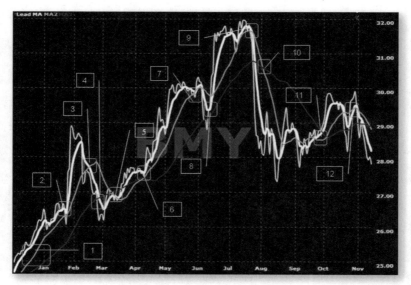

FIGURE 4.3   Chart of BMY—12 Key Points

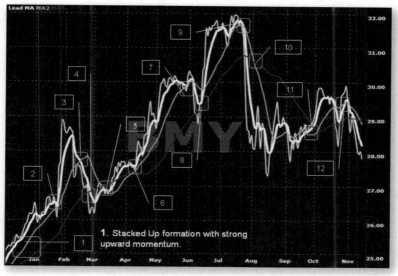

FIGURE 4.4   Chart of BMY—#1

1. In Figure 4.4, M1 (white) turns up and crosses M2 (green) and M3 (blue). The MAs are stacked up. This is strong continuing upward momentum.

2. In Figure 4.5, M1 (white) points down sharply toward M2 (green). At this point, we are watching for the crossover of M2 (green) and expect the cycle to reverse. However, M1 (white) does not cross over M2 (green). This indicates a continued rising cycle, which is

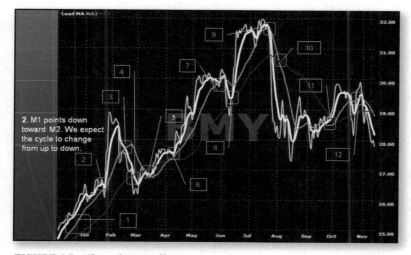

FIGURE 4.5   Chart of BMY—#2

FIGURE 4.6 Chart of BMY—#3

called continuation. Note: Continuation of a previous cycle is a very important characteristic to watch for with M1. This is momentum continuing.

3. In Figure 4.6, M1 (white) again points down sharply toward M2 (green). At this point, we are watching for the crossover of M2 (green) and expect the cycle to reverse. M1 (white) crosses M2 (green) and is pointing down. Bias is now strongly down. We are now watching as M2 begins to roll over and head toward M3. M3 begins to roll over, and we expect a possible stacked-down formation. This does not happen as M1 turns back up and heads back toward M2.

4. In Figure 4.7, M1 (white) crosses M3 (blue). However, MAs are *not* stacked down at this point. M2 has not yet crossed M3. To be stacked, all must be in this exact order: M1, M2, and M3.

5. In Figure 4.8, M1 (white) crosses M2 (green), then M3 (blue). However, MAs are not stacked up at this point. M2 (green) is still below M3 (blue). We are watching to see if M1 continues to move upward and whether M2 turns up to follow M1. M1 has gone through its birth phase, momentum phase, and exhaustion phase, to death phase and is about to enter a new birth phase.

6. In Figure 4.9, M1 (white) rolls down toward M2 (green). M2 (green) crosses M3 (blue), and M1 (white) is pointing up dramatically. MAs

FIGURE 4.7 Chart of BMY—#4

are now stacked up. Note the crossover of M2 to M3, which is a very important crossover to watch. When this crossover happens—the beginning of the stacked-up formation—it indicates very strong upward momentum. This is also an example of the momentum phase weakening, going into exhaustion, and then returning back into momentum. It is also called continuation.

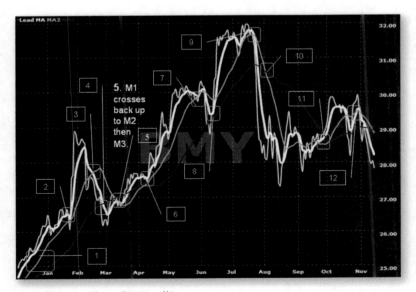

FIGURE 4.8 Chart of BMY—#5

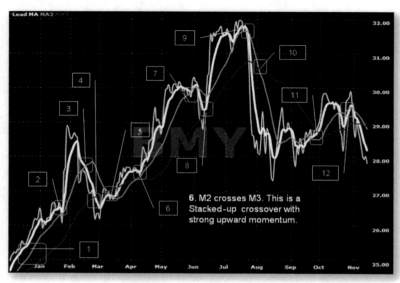

FIGURE 4.9   Chart of BMY—#6

7. In Figure 4.10, lead MA M1 (white) points down sharply toward
   M2 (green) and just touches M2. This is a sign of exhaustion and
   possibly death. Because of the dramatic stacked-up formation, we
   are aware of another possible continuation of M1. M1 rolls up, but
   only briefly.

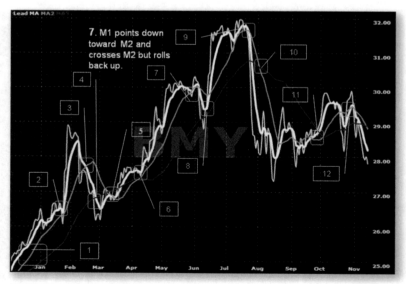

FIGURE 4.10   Chart of BMY—#7

8. In Figure 4.11, M1 (white) turns up toward M2 (green). However, MAs are *not* stacked down at this point. M2 has not crossed M3 yet. To be stacked, all MAs must be in an exact order: M1, M2, and M3. We are watching to see if M1 returns to the momentum phase and crosses M2. M1 eventually crosses M2, and BMY returns to a stacked-up formation with strong upward momentum.

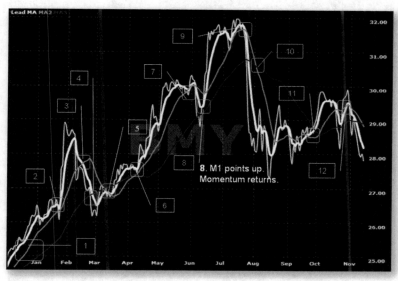

FIGURE 4.11 Chart of BMY—#8

9. In Figure 4.12, M1 (white) turns down. Momentum is returning but not confirmed. MAs are not stacked. We watch as M2 turns down and follows M1. We expect M2 to continue down and cross M3.

10. In Figure 4.13, M1 (white) points down sharply toward M2 (green) and crosses it. The birth of a new cycle, started at #9, is followed by momentum. Momentum is confirmed with the crossover of M2 to M3 and the formation of a stacked-down cycle.

   The crossover of M2 to M3 is an important one to be aware of because stacked-down formations confirm and validate momentum.

11. In Figure 4.14, M1 (white) turns upward toward M2 (green) and crosses MA3 (blue). After M1 crosses M3, M1 turns up dramatically, and we expect M2 to turn up and follow M1. With the crossover of M2 to M3, the cycle returns to a stacked-up formation.

FIGURE 4.12   Chart of BMY—#9

FIGURE 4.13   Chart of BMY—#10

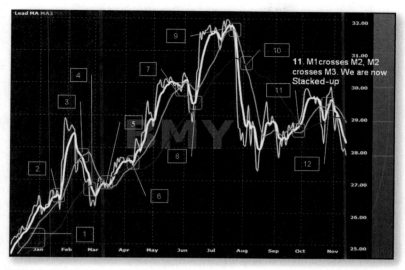

FIGURE 4.14   Chart of BMY—#11

12. In Figure 4.15, M1 (white) turns down and heads toward M2 (green). M1 (white) continues dramatically down as M2 (green) turns down and follows M1. M2 (green) crosses M3 (blue), and the cycle returns to a stacked-down formation with strong downward momentum.

Every stock, index, or exchange-traded fund cycles through the 12 key points noted on the BMY chart. These are examples of the four phases of a cycle. We must train our eyes to identify these four phases. We discuss entry and exit rules based on these points a little later in Chapter 6.

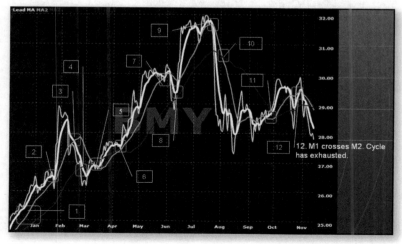

FIGURE 4.15   Chart of BMY—#12

Supplementary Moving Averages

We place two supplementary MAs on the chart for the purposes of under-standing the long-term trend of the stock. In order to understand cycles, we must understand the power of the trend indicators. The sum total of repeating cycles defines a trend direction of a stock. The saying that "The trend is your friend" is very true. We must learn to trade with the trend, not against it.

Moving Average 4—M4 (White)

M4 (white) is the fourth moving average and represented by the thinner white line on the chart in Figure 4.16. This line will always be more hori-zontal] or be gently trending up or gently trending down. This indicator plots the average price of a security over a long period, with all data given equal weight in the average.

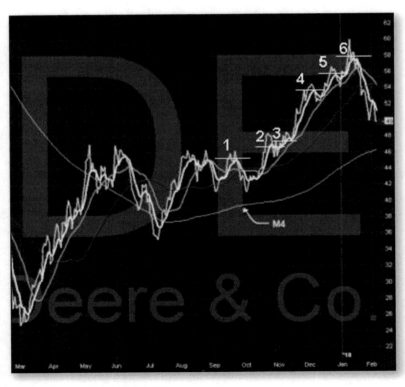

FIGURE 4.16 Chart of DE—M4

M4 (white) is used to identify the trend direction of the security. If the price tic, M1 (white), M2 (green), and M3 (blue) are cycling above M4 (white), this generally indicates an up-trending stock. If the M4 (white) trend line is above M1 (white), M2 (green), and M3 (blue), this indicates a downward-trending stock.

The DE chart shows M4 (thinner white line) trending upward in September. Note M1 as it cycles up higher. These repeating upward cycles are defining the direction of the M4 trend line. Also note the higher highs and higher lows of M1. There is a direct relationship of a dramatic upward or downward M4 trend line and the higher highs and lower highs of M1 as it cycles up and down.

Trusting M1 (white) as it cycles up and down is absolutely vital to understanding cycles and trends. You will never reach your full potential as an Advanced Charting trader unless you trust M1.

Note: As M1 cycles up and down with higher highs and higher lows or lower highs and lower lows, each new birth to death phase of the cycle forecasts a future cycle.

The correct pattern recognition, understanding, and interpretation of Window 1—Chart 1, Window 2—Chart 2, and their lower indicators will give Advanced Charting traders phenomenal control to know when to enter, exit, and wait to trade. This will be discussed in greater detail throughout the next several chapters.

Notice the higher highs and higher lows of M1 as it rolls higher with each cycle, #1 through #6, on the chart in Figure 4.16. Also note the longer up cycles followed by shorter down cycles of M1. This clearly shows an up-trending stock as the price tic moves higher with each cycle.

Chart of DE—M1 (White), M2 (Green), M3 (Blue), and M4 (White)

On the chart of DE in Figure 4.17, note that the positions of the moving averages and the stock price are all above M4 (white). Note the upward angle of M4 (white). It is easy to see the general upward trend of DE over the one-year timeline. Also note where the stock price in mid-July rolled over and went stacked down. This strong deep down cycle caused M4 to begin to change its path. This is a sign of upward-cycle weakness in the current and possibly future cycles.

BENDING M4

FIGURE 4.17 Chart of DE—M4 Bending

The bending of M4 is a key indicator to watch. Will M4 continue to bend flat and then down? Will the price tic break through the M4 support level? Will the moving averages begin to cycle under M4? These are questions that you should begin to ask yourself when you analyze this chart.

The price tic breaking through the M4 support level in August is a key indicator of a possible change in the trend of DE.

Chart of C—Lead MA M1 (White), M2 (Green), M3 (Blue), M4 (White)

The chart of C in Figure 4.18 is another example of the stock price and moving averages crossing over and under M4 (white). Note the dramatic decline of this stock and the validation of the downward trend by the crossovers of all the moving averages.

FIGURE 4.18   Chart of C—M4 Bending

Note the position of the moving averages and the stock price all above M4 (white) in January. Also note the upward-slopping angle of M4 (white). It is easy to see the general upward trend of C over this time period. Also note where the stock price in March rolled over and went through M4. This is the first sign of a possible change in the trend. In July, M1 again broke through M4 support and went stacked down under M4. This is confirmation of the possible change in the trend line. In August, M1 (white) began to cycle under M4. This strong deep down cycle caused M4 to begin to change its path and begin to arch downward.

Moving Average—M5 (Purple)

The fifth and last moving average indicator is the M5 (purple). This indicator plots the average price of a security over a very long period, with all data given equal weight in the average. On the C chart in Figure 4.19, a one-year chart, we can see the purple M5 MA line is almost horizontal across the chart. When a chart of a shorter time period, such as one year, six months, or three months, does not show the M5 (purple), the stock is trading either extremely high above or below the present M5 (purple). Such a chart also can suggest that the stock is relatively new and there isn't enough history gathered to create the M5 indicator. To see a broader view of the chart to determine where the stock is trading relative to the M5, move out to a one-year or two-year view. These wider views are used especially for LEAPS trading.

FIGURE 4.19 Chart of C—M4, M5

Now that we have reviewed all of the moving average indicators`and understand their relationships one to another, it is important to review again cycles and trends.

1. Cycles are defined by the movement of the price tic, M1, M2, and M3, moving into and out of stacked formations.
2. Cycles are entering the momentum phase when M1 turns up or down dramatically followed by M2.
3. A cycle enters into a strong momentum phase when M2 crosses M3 and all three MAs are in a stacked formation.
4. A cycle may be entering exhaustion when M1 turns toward M2.
5. A cycle has entered the death phase when M1 and M2 are both in agreement and headed in the same direction.

Note: Do not enter or exit positions just on these cycle characteristics of Window 1—Chart 1, a topic that is explained in more depth in chapter 6. To ensure correct entry and exit of all positions, it is vital to apply the information provided by the lower indicators.

CHAPTER 5

Bollinger Bands, PSAR, Channels, Zones, and FTL

The Bollinger band (BB) is another very important technical indicator. It is represented by the red lines on the chart in Figure 5.1. The bands are plotted at two standard deviations above and below M2 (green). When using two standard deviations, we know that 95 percent of the price data (the line chart of the stock) will fall between the two Bollinger bands. In this chapter we study in greater detail how the line chart will travel between the Bollinger bands and M1 (white) and why this is a vital indicator to increase our profits.

- There are two bands or lines placed around a moving average (MA).

- The bands are placed two standard deviations above and below M2. Two deviations ensure that 95 percent of the price data will fall within the two bands.

- When the stock price touches the upper band, the stock is considered overbought, and the price is expected to drop. When the stock price touches the lower band, the stock is considered oversold, and the price is expected to rise.

- If the price crosses over M2 (green), the opposite band becomes a price target.

- In a strong uptrend, the price will fluctuate between the upper band and M1 (white). In a strong down trend, the price will fluctuate between the lower band and M1 (white).

In Figure 5.1, the upper red line is called the upper BB (or UBB). The lower red line is called the lower BB (or LBB). Keep in mind that only 5 percent of the price move of the stock occurs outside either of these bands. That means that 95 percent of the stock movement occurs between these two red lines. Note that the tic went outside the Bollinger bands only nine times in six months.

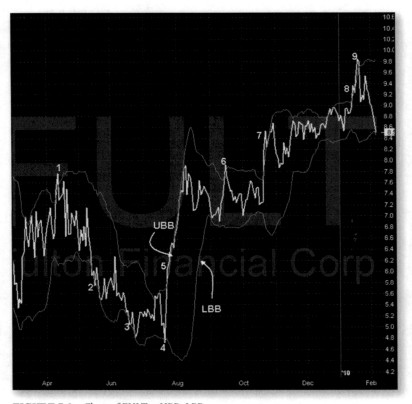

FIGURE 5.1 Chart of FULT—UBB, LBB

The Bollinger band indicator provides a quick picture of where the stock price is relative to its overall cycle. This does not mean that if the price tic is at the LBB we should enter a new position or if it is at the UBB we should tethered slingshot (TSS). The price tic can be at the UBB or LBB, and the stock could continue to move upward or downward. Therefore, we must use our MAs and lower indicators with the Bollinger bands. Other technical indicators, which we study later in this chapter, will verify this. Bollinger bands also show another very important indicator: volatility.

As standard deviation is a measure of volatility, Bollinger bands adjust themselves to market conditions. When the market becomes more volatile, the bands widen and move farther away from M2 (green). During less volatile periods, the bands contract, moving closer to M2 (green). Traders often use the tightening of the bands, which creates a pinch, as an early indication that the volatility is about to increase sharply. The pinch is often an indication of a change in the cycle.

Also, it is important to note that the stock price in a strong uptrend will hug the UBB. In a strong downtrend, the stock price will hug the LBB. These are important characteristics to identify, as they allow us to stay in a position (10-cent rule) for greater profits when the stock is strongly increasing or to stay in a TSS for greater profits when the stock is strongly decreasing. The stock price tick hugging the Bollinger band and being supported or resisted by M1 (white) is one factor we use to identify the false V. In Figure 5.2, notice the false Vs occurring when the stock is hugging the UBB or LBB as discussed later in this chapter.

The "hippo" is an amazing technical indicator. Why? It was formulated to create a "visual" of strength or weakness of resistance and support but more importantly to give the trader the ability to "see" three important developments unfold. 1. A "pinch" occurs when the upper and lower bands begin to turn towards each other to form a compression. When this happens, we know that a "flare" will soon occur. 2. A flare occurs when both the upper and lower bands begin to turn away from each other and begin to flare open. This indicates that volume is increasing and that resistance and support are moving further apart. This is followed often times by a hippo. 3. A hippo occurs when the upper and lower bands keep flaring farther apart from each other. This is a sign that there is very strong "momentum" and volume occurring. Applying the methodologies of Advanced Charting—and using the "hippo" as an important indicator—very profitable trades are realized by knowing that momentum is continuing with strength. After a hippo has formed and one of the bands turns to follows the direction of the opposite band—a trader can expect tremendous movement in the stock.

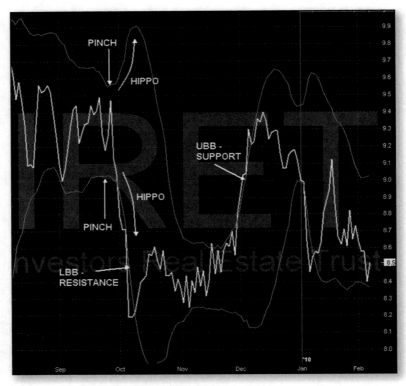

FIGURE 5.2 Chart of IRET—Support, Resistance

■ PSAR

In Advanced Charting on Window 1—Chart 1, the PSAR indicator is turned on as a default indicator. It can be unchecked to turn it off, if we need to remove the indicator for more clarity of reading the chart.

PSAR stands for parabolic stop and reversal. Advanced Charting does not use this definition. The sole purpose of the newly formulated Advanced Charting PSAR is to identify a lower indicator crossover of red line to blue line. When an arrow appears either red or blue, a crossover has occurred in one or more of the lower indicators. The basic crossover is an important technical indicator, and an arrow is a pay-attention indicator.

We do not place a trade on PSAR, as this indicator is intended only to be an alert indicator that a crossover has occurred. There are many subtleties to be aware of when reviewing the lower indicators to gauge the importance of the appearance of the PSAR arrow.

If the PSAR indicator is triggered, a yellow dot first appears. If the new direction of M1 (white) is true, an arrow appears. Once the arrow appears, it is followed by more yellow dots. If a new cycle has developed, a series of dots appears, pulls away from the previous dots, and moves either up or down, depending on the direction of the cycle. This movement confirms and validates that a new cycle has developed.

The more dramatically the dots move up or down in either direction, the stronger the momentum moving in that direction. PSAR tracks the long and short legs of the Vs and M1 and ignores all false Vs.

Again, we do not trade with PSAR but use this indicator to identify that a crossover has occurred. It is one more indicator to validate and confirm true or false Vs.

On the chart in Figure 5.3, note the green arrow and the upward bias cycle beginning in early August and the series of yellow dots through mid-September. Note the many false Vs that occurred, but PSAR ignored them, confirming and validating continued upward momentum.

FIGURE 5.3 Chart of AMD—PSAR

The appearance of the arrow in either direction is a sign to pay attention and watch for more confirmation that a new birth phase of a cycle has begun.

We study how PSAR responds to various changes of the price tic as a stock cycles up and down in greater detail in this chapter.

Upward bias exists when . . .

■ The stock price (tic) is trading above PSAR—the stock is generally cycling up and bias is therefore up.

■ The yellow dots move higher than the previous dot, and momentum is building.

■ The dots spread out from one to another, indicating and confirming momentum.

On the chart in Figure 5.4, note the red arrow and downward bias cycle beginning in early September and the series of yellow dots to mid-October. Note the many false Vs that occurred, but PSAR ignored them, confirming and validating continued downward momentum.

The appearance of the arrow in either direction is a sign to pay attention and watch for more confirmation that a new birth phase of a cycle has begun.

FIGURE 5.4 Chart of AMD—PSAR

We study how PSAR responds to various changes of the price tic as a stock cycles up and down in greater detail in this chapter. Downward bias exists when:

- The stock price (tic) is trading below PSAR—the stock is generally cycling down, and bias is therefore down.

- The yellow dots move lower than the previous dot, and momentum is bias down.

- The dots spread out from one to another, confirming downward bias.

■ Channel Indicators: C1, C2, C3

Drawing the parallel straight-line channel indicator to identify support and resistance for a security has been an important tool for Compound Stock Earnings (CSE). It is the simplest method to help traders identify the lower 25 percent and upper 75 percent area of a stock's cycle.

CSE has used the hand-drawn straight-line channel indicator to establish bias of the trend successfully for years. The human element, however, can present challenges for many traders who do not know where to draw the first line. The decision can be subjective and biased. However, with straight-line parallel channels, we do not need an exact position of the lines, only a general direction of the trend.

To remove the human element and improve the accuracy of the parallel channel indicator, a new channel indicator was formulated to confirm and validate the direction of the cycle and therefore the overall trend. Advanced charting parallel channels are determined by tracking the long and short legs of the price tic and the extreme highs and lows of the modified candlewicks. This combined formula establishes the direction of the channel, which is the direction of the current cycle, and establishes true points of support and resistance.

The channel indicator was formatted specifically for Advanced Charting to identify cycle support and resistance points. It is a valuable indicator for trading covered calls, LEAPS, and credit spreads when used in conjunction with the Bollinger bands.

The channels shown on the chart in Figure 5.5 track the movement of the daily price tic. A series of price tics moving up or down will determine a point to break the path and change direction, turning the channels up, down, or flat. If a series of up tics with long up-leg Vs breaks through resistance, the channels will break their path, change direction, and turn upward. This change indicates a new direction of the next cycle.

FIGURE 5.5 Chart of ALL—Channels

The same applies to a series of down tics with long down-leg Vs. When this happens and the price tic breaks through support, the channel line, C2, will reposition its path and change from upward to a downward direction. C1 and C3 will position themselves according to the highest high and lowest low of the modified candle wicks.

We do not place trades with channels but use them only to visualize the cycle and its direction. As the price tic advances up or down toward C1, C2, and C3, these various points are critical resistance and support points and must be respected.

The channel lines are mathematically determined by the movement of the price tic. The movement of the price tic establishes the direction or angle of the channels. A series of price moves in a given direction will establish the C2 line. From this line, both C1 and C2 lines are determined. C1 defines resistance of the pattern based on the highest price points during the period. It most likely appears much higher than the tic based on close prices versus highest intraday trades. C1 is the highest potential price at expiration based on the current pattern. If the index breaks the pattern, we have strategies to manage the position. As the price tic moves closer to C1 resistance, the other indicators may show the probabilities of the tic breaking through C1.

■ Zones

Earlier we discussed that the price tic will cycle up and down between the UBB and LBB. As the tic moves through its cycles, it moves closer to C1 or closer to C3. As this happens, zones are created by major points of support and resistance. A zone is the area between C1 and UBB, UBB and M1, M1 and LBB, and LBB and C3.

Figure 5.6 illustrates the four zones in the current cycle starting in mid-January. If we look back in history to November as the price tic and M1 moved higher and lower, the zones changed in width. The four zones got wider or narrower as the price tic cycled up and down.

FIGURE 5.6   Chart of OEX—Zones

The channel indicator and the zones can help credit spread traders to see the probabilities of where the price tic may move to by the Friday target line or by expiration Friday. The Advanced Charting channel lines define true extreme levels of support and resistance. We know the probabilities of how high and how low the price tic may move during the current cycle of the stock or index. The tic either stays in a zone or moves out and into the next zone. The channels lines identify the four trading zones.

Zone 1—The area between the UBB and the highest channel line called C1.
Zone 2—The area between M1 and the UBB.
Zone 3—The area between M1 and the LBB.
Zone 4—The area between the LBB and the lower channel line called C3.

How do we use the zones to improve our credit spread entries and exits? We know the price tic moves up and down in cycles. At the market close on February 7, 2010, the tic for OEX is in Zone 3, between M1 and the LBB. This zone is tight, or close together. Because M1 is dramatically down, the probability is very high for an inverted V on Monday. Or the tic may advance lower and could enter into Zone 4 (between the LBB and C3). If M1 remains dramatically down, the tic eventually will move into Zone 4. Because Zone 4 is so tight, the tic could break below C3. Should this happen, the next support level is M4. If the tic breaks below C3 support, a new set of channels will be drawn and OEX will continue to cycle downward. Or if M1 turns flat to slightly up, the tic will remain in Zone 3 by Friday. By trusting M1 and understanding the relationship of M1 to the other moving averages, we can predict with a high degree of accuracy which zone the tic will be in at the Friday target line.

A trader's knowledge of these zones and of the probability of the tic remaining in or moving out of a zone and into a higher or lower zone will help him or her in entering new credit spread trades.

Upper Bollinger Band and C1

Both the upper Bollinger band (UBB) and C1 are important points of resistance. However, C1 is the most important resistance line. Selecting a short strike above the UBB and below C1 for a call spread ensures that, based on history, it is unlikely that the index will move to that price.

There are, however, many subtleties that must be considered. Ideally, the short strike of a call spread will be above the UBB and as close to C1 as possible. This zone is the sweet spot because the chart pattern indicates a low chance of the price tic moving there. Note: Understanding the spread of the Bollinger bands is also critical in determining the zone and sweet spot. The spread of the Bollinger bands is the distance between the upper and lower bands, whether they are pinching toward each other or opening up from each other.

Lower Bollinger Band and C3

Both the lower Bollinger band (LBB) and C3 are important points of support. However, C3 is the most important support line. C3 is support based on the lowest intraday price points during the time period being evaluated. Put spreads should always be more conservative than call spreads, so ideally the short put strike should be outside (below) the LBB or between the LBB and C3. The zone or sweet spot is the area between the channels and the Bollinger bands.

Note the C2 channel line will act as resistance or support, depending on where the price tic is relative to being above or below it. The C1 and C2 channel lines are typically closer together. A credit spread trade constructed between C1 and C2 or C2 and C3 would be considered a very high risk trade and is not advisable.

■ Friday Target Line

Advanced charting is the only charting program that I know of with a target line showing a future date. This line is called the Friday target line, or FTL. The purpose of the FTL is to show a fixed target as the price tic and the technical indicators move forward from one trading day to the next, getting closer to the FTL.

The chart in Figure 5.7 shows a dashed vertical gray line followed by a series of light gray solid vertical lines. The light gray solid vertical lines are all the Fridays of the month. The light gray vertical line at the extreme far right of each chart is the next Friday date.

The figure shows the closing of the market on January 25, 2010, and the next FTL of January 29, 2010 (the light gray vertical line to the right of the price tic). The interpretation of the Advanced Charting

61

BOLLINGER BANDS, PSAR, CHANNELS, ZONES, AND FTL

indicators shows the probability of where the price tic may close by the next Friday date.

FIGURE 5.7   Chart of HOT—Friday Target Line

Trusting M1 (white) and understanding how to interpret all of the indicators in an exact order enable traders to forecast the probability of where the price tic will be by Friday. The FTL is especially helpful for trading weekly credit spreads and LEAPS trades.

CHAPTER 6

Putting It All Together: MAs and the BBs

T hus far we have studied all of the upper chart indicators. Let us now review them and put them all together.

Figure 6.1 shows the relationship of the line chart, M1, M2, M3, and the Bollinger bands (BBs). Once you have looked at hundreds, if not

FIGURE 6.1   Chart of CCL—MAs and BBs Stacked Up

thousands, of charts, you will begin to recognize exactly what these technical indicators mean.

Note that in mid-March, M1 turns up and crosses over M2. M2 turns up and follows M1 and crosses M3. The stacked-up formation indicates strong upward momentum.

The reverse applies when we are managing a tethered slingshot (TSS)[1]. In Figure 6.2, note that, in mid-September, M1 flattens out and turns down toward M2. M1 continues on and crosses M2. M2 turns and follows M1, and continues on to cross M3. CCL is now stacked down with strong downward momentum. M3 turns and follows M2, confirming and validating this downward cycle, and indicates an excellent TSS.

FIGURE 6.2 Chart of CCL—MAs and BBs Stacked Down

In mid-March, the chart in Figure 6.3 shows a green PSAR arrow followed by a series of yellow dots moving up and spacing out. When the

[1] *Covered Calls and LEAPS—A Wealth Option: A Guide for Generating Extraordinary Monthly Income.* Joseph R. Hooper, Aaron R. Zalweski, and Robert Kiyosaki. Hoboken, NJ: Wiley, 2006.

green arrow appears, we know that a crossover of red to blue has occurred on one or more of the lower indicator. PSAR confirms and validates upward momentum.

FIGURE 6.3 Chart of CCL—MAs and BBs PSAR Up

In mid-September, the chart in Figure 6.4 shows a red PSAR arrow followed by a series of yellow dots moving down and spacing out. When the red arrow appears, we know that a crossover of red to blue has occurred on one or more of the lower indicators. PSAR confirms and validates downward momentum.

In mid-February, the chart in Figure 6.5 shows M1 turning up, and the tic is near the upper BB (UBB). Parallel channels C1, C2, and C3 appear. The channels begin to define the direction of the current cycle and will remain in this direction until the price tic breaks through resistance or support. There must be a series of price tics moving beyond C1 or C3 before a new set of channels is drawn. Note the channel lines changing in May and June.

FIGURE 6.4   Chart of CCL—MAs and BBs PSAR Down

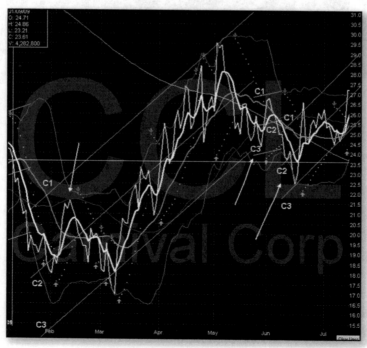

FIGURE 6.5   Chart of CCL—MAs, BBs, and Channels

■ Window 1—Chart 1

Chart 1 is the most important chart. It is the first chart that we analyze before we look at any other indicator. You must review the indicators on this chart in a precise and exact order and must follow this order with every chart that we review. Your discipline to do this will help identify the many subtleties that exist with advanced charting. Your skill level will improve as you enter and exit trades with precision and are able to predict the future as M1 cycles up and down.

Window 1—Chart 1 Analysis

Refer to Figure 6.6.

FIGURE 6.6   Chart of CAT—Specific Order to Review

1. **M1.** Look at M1 first. What is the angle? Is it turned up, flat, or down? Study to see if M1 is slightly up or down or dramatically up or down. This is extremely important. Where are the highs and lows of M1?
2. **Price tic.** Where is the tic? Is it turned up or down?
3. **M2.** Where is M2 relative to M1? Is M1 above M2 or below M2?
4. **M3.** Where is M3 relative to M2? Is M3 above M2 or below M2? Is it stacked up or down?

5. **UBB.** Where is the UBB? Is it turned down, turned up, or flat?
6. **LBB.** Where is the LBB? Is it turned down, turned up, or flat?
7. **Pinch.** Is the pinch a flare or a hippo? A flare is when both the upper and lower bands begin to turn away from each other and flare open, and a hippo is when the upper and lower bands keep flaring farther apart from each other.
8. **C1.** Is the price tic at C1?
9. **C2.** Is the price tic at C2?
10. **C3.** Is the price tic at C3?
11. **PSAR.** Is there a red or green arrow? Are there any yellow dots forming a pattern?
12. **Bias.** What is the bias of the cycle?
13. **M4.** What is the bias of the trend?
14. **M5.** What is the bias of M5?

Our objective in answering these questions is to arrive at an opinion of the bias of the cycle and the trend. Is the bias of the cycle up, down, or flat? Is the bias of the trend up, down, or flat?

Do not look at anything but Window 1—Chart 1 during this first analysis; it contains the key elements of charting you need to determine the bias of cycles and trends.

Our answers to questions #1 through #12 will enable us to form an opinion of the bias of the cycle. Our answer to question #13 will enable us to form an opinion of the bias for the trend. We cannot apply the power of advanced charting unless we determine the bias of Chart 1 and can answer the two bias questions.

During this review, do not look at any of the other indicators or Chart 2. This is extremely important. Why? Thousands of subtleties exist from one stock or index chart to another. It would be impossible to learn these subtle indicator changes without reviewing charts in an exact and precise order every time.

You must familiarize yourself with the review of all of the indicators by looking at literally hundreds of charts. Soon you will begin to read with complete confidence exactly what these technical indicators mean and are forecasting for us.

Next we review the CAT chart in Figure 5.7 in the exact and precise order as described. Use this format throughout your chart reviews.

1. M1 is turned down dramatically.
2. The tic has V'd down and is under C2 resistance.
3. M2 is above M1.
4. M3 is above M2. Stacked down.
5. UBB is turned down.
6. LBB is down.
7. A pinch formed in January and flared with a hippo.
8. C1 is down.
9. C2 is resistance.
10. C3 is support.
11. A PSAR red arrow appears with stepping-down dots.
12. Bias of the cycle is down stacked down.
13. M4 is dramatically up with a slight bend in mid-January.
14. M5 is flat.

Now that you have an opinion on bias of the cycle and trend, you can analyze the lower indicators to build a case to support your opinion. The lower indicators will or will not confirm and validate that opinion. With these data, you will make your decision to trade or wait.

CHAPTER 7

Lower Chart Indicators L1 through L4

Moving average (MA) indicators are lagging indicators. They are lagging because the data are based on past history over a set number of periods or days. Regardless of this, MA settings are very important in terms of validating the V. The position of the MAs determines 90 percent of what we do when trading covered calls and LEAPS following the Compound Stock Earnings (CSE) methodology.

As we discussed earlier, M1 (white) is the lead dog. When M1 (white) is dramatically up or down, a strong cycle is occurring in either direction, and therefore we can trade positions fairly easily by applying our CSE management rules. However, we know that M1 (white) will change direction as the stock cycles up and down. Therefore, M1 (white) will regularly turn flat or horizontal. When M1 (white) begins to roll over from its upward or downward position to a flat or horizontal position, the highs and lows are averaging out. Other technical indicators must be applied to interpret the probabilities of the next cycle direction.

Look at the chart of CCL in late January shown in Figure 7.1. Note that M1 (white) has flattened out and gone horizontal. When this happens, we need to use our other lower chart indicators to interpret the probabilities of the next price direction. Note all of the arrows indicating a flat to slightly up or down M1. A slightly up or slightly down M1 is basically the same as a true flat or horizontal M1.

FIGURE 7.1 Chart of CCL—M1 Flat

Look at chart in Figure 7.2. At the bottom of the chart are four key indicators that are used to determine likely future price direction of the stock.

When M1 (white) flattens out and we examine the current position of the chart, we see three things:

1. An inverted V has formed on the chart.
2. M1 (white) has flattened out and gone horizontal.
3. The lower indicators are pointing down.

All four lower indicators have moved from the top of their scales (scales are the vertical numbers on the right edge of the indicators) and have turned down. The red line has crossed through the blue line. This gives us strong indication that the inverted V is valid and bias for the stock price in the short term is down. We do not tethered slingshot here but wait for more confirmation and validation.

The next section discusses these indicators and how we use them.

ADVANCED CHARTING TECHNIQUES FOR HIGH PROBABILITY TRADING

FIGURE 7.2 Chart of CCL—Lower Indicators

■ Defining the Lower Chart Indicators

As mentioned, there are four lower chart indicators that we use primarily to get an understanding of bias when M1 (white) flattens out and goes horizontal. In this section, we define and explain these indicators. In the next section, we look at several examples of M1 (white) flattening out and how we use these indicators to confirm and validate our opinion of bias.

It's very important to note that none of these lower chart indicators is used alone. We view all four indicators together to get a better idea of bias for the stock.

Lower Indicator 1—L1

Lower indicator 1 (L1) is a trend following the momentum indicator that shows the relationship between two moving averages of prices. It is the first lower chart technical indicator that we check when M1 (white) is flat. Lower indicator 1 is displayed at the bottom of Figure 7.3.

FIGURE 7.3 Chart of CCL—L1

Upward bias exists when:

1. The red line turns up toward the blue line from the lower region of the L1 scale. When we see this happening from the lower region of the L1 scale, we are watching for a change in cycle.

2. The red line continues up and crosses over the blue line from the bottom of the lower region of the L1 scale.
3. The red line has crossed over the blue and continues to travel above the blue line.

Downward bias exists when:

1. The red line turns down toward the blue line from the upper region of the L1 scale. When we see this happening from the upper region of the L1 scale, we are watching for a change in cycle.
2. The red line continues down and crosses over the blue line from the top upper region of the L1 scale.
3. The red line has crossed over the blue line and continues to travel below it.

The red line tracks the price tic. The blue line is called the signal line, and its direction is influenced by the daily movement of the price tic. L1, in this example, shows the red and blue lines high relative to the scale on the right. The blue signal line still can move upward, but there is more room for L1 to move downward toward the bottom of the scale. Note the movement of L1 up and down and the movement of M1 on the chart. When M1 and the price tic move downward, L1 also moves down. When the price tic moves upward, L1 will begin to move up as well.

L1 is the most important lower indicator of the indicators under Chart 1 and the first of the lower indicators.

We discuss the use of this indicator in more detail later in the chapter when we review chart examples of M1 (white) flattening out and discuss how to use the lower indicators to understand likely stock price direction.

Where is L1 relative to its scale? Is it high, low, or in the middle? Note that if L1 is low relative to its scale, the cycle on Chart 1 is low. If L1 is high relative to its scale, the cycle on Chart 1 is high. **L1 is very accurate in determining probable direction of the next cycle.**

Lower Indicator 2—L2

Lower indicator 2 (L2) is a momentum indicator that shows the location of the current close price relative to the high/low range over a set number of periods. Lower indicator 2 is displayed in the lower region of Figure 7.4.

FIGURE 7.4   Chart of CCL—L2

Lower indicator 2 oscillates between a range of 0 and 100. Readings below 20 are generally considered oversold (bias is therefore up), and readings above 80 are generally considered overbought (bias is therefore down).

However, when interpreting lower indicator 2, it is important to understand that a stock regularly will continue to rise after the L2 has reached 80 and regularly will continue to fall after L2 has reached 20. As such, when using L2, we are looking for the oscillator to move from overbought territory back below 80 and from oversold territory back above 20. As with the other technical indicators, we use the L2 when M1 (white) is flat, slightly up, or down.

Upward bias exists when:

1. L2 is in the oversold region (20) and is turning up or has crossed over the 20 line.
2. L2 is moving in a direction from the bottom of the scale to the top.
3. L2 is hovering near or above the overbought area (80) and is yet to turn down and cross 80.

Downward bias exists when:

1. L2 moves from the overbought area (greater than 80) to below 80.
2. L2 is moving in a direction from the top of its scale to the bottom.
3. L2 is hovering in the oversold area below M2 (green) and is yet to turn up and cross M2 (green).

We discuss the use of this indicator in more detail later in the chapter when we review chart examples of M1 (white) flattening out and discuss how to use the lower indicators to understand likely stock price direction.

The blue line is the signal line, and its path up or down is created by the movement of the red line. If the signal line is pointed up, momentum is still upward. If the signal line is pointed down, momentum is downward. The direction of the signal line can be used to determine if a cycle is still in its momentum phase.

Lower Indicator 3—L3

Lower indicator 3 (L3) is another momentum oscillator used to compare the magnitude of a stock's recent gains to the magnitude of its recent losses and turns that information into a number that ranges from 0 to 100. Readings below 30 are generally considered oversold (bias is therefore up), and readings above 70 are generally considered overbought (bias is therefore down).

When interpreting L3, as with L2, it is important to understand that a stock regularly will continue to rise after it has reached 70 and may continue to fall after it has reached 30. As such, when using L3, we are looking for the oscillator to move from overbought territory back below 70 and from oversold territory back above 30. As with the other techni-cal indicators, we use L3 when M1 (white) flattens out (see Figure 7.5).

Upward bias exists when:

1. L3 is in the oversold region (below 30) and is turning up or has crossed over the 30 line.
2. L3 is moving in a direction from the bottom of the L3 scale to the top.

Downward bias exists when:

1. L3 moves from the overbought area (greater than 70) to below 70.
2. L3 is moving in a direction from the top of the scale to the bottom.

FIGURE 7.5 Chart of CCL – L3

We discuss the use of this indicator later in the chapter when we review chart examples of the M1 (white) flattening out and discuss how to use the lower indicators to understand likely stock price direction.

Lower Indicator 4—L4

Lower indicator 4 (L4) is a volume indicator that adds a period's volume when the closing price is up and subtracts the period's volume when the closing price is down. A cumulative total of the volume additions and subtractions forms the L4 line. The idea behind L4 is that changes in the volume will precede price changes—increases in volume often indicate the presence of smart money flowing into a security. L4 is thus a *leading* indicator tracking smart money.

A rising L4 line indicates that the volume is heavier on up days. If the price also is rising, the L4 can serve as a confirmation of the price uptrend.

ADVANCED CHARTING TECHNIQUES FOR HIGH PROBABILITY TRADING

In such a case, the rising price is the result of an increased demand for the security, which is a requirement of a healthy uptrend.

However, if prices are moving higher while the volume line is dropping, a negative divergence is present. This divergence suggests that the uptrend is not healthy and should be taken as a warning signal that the trend will not persist.

The numerical value of L4 is not important; the direction of the line is. Concentrate on the L4 direction and its relationship with the security's price (see Figure 7.6).

FIGURE 7.6   Chart of CCL – L4

Upward bias exists when:

1. The red line has crossed the blue line and is heading upward, indicating that volume is heavier on up days.
2. The red line is moving up and away from the blue line. This indicates that smart money is moving into the position rapidly.

Downward bias exists when:

1. The red line has crossed the blue line and is heading downward, indicating that volume is lower on down days.
2. The red line is moving down and away from the blue line. This indicates that smart money is moving out of the position rapidly.

Use the lower indicators when the lead MA (white) flattens out.

Now that we understand all our moving average indicators and the lower chart indicators, it is time to put all this information together. As discussed, when we have a clear cycle direction where M1 (white) is pointing dramatically up or down, it is very easy to interpret the direction of the stock price. However, when M1 (white) is flat or horizontal, we need to assess our lower chart indicators to understand bias.

There are three basic conditions where M1 (white) is flat:

1. M1 (white) has been declining and is now flattening out.
2. M1 (white) has been rising and is now flattening out.
3. M1 (white) and M2 (green) have converged and are moving together horizontally.

Next we present examples of each of these conditions and show how to use the lower chart indicators to interpret the probabilities of stock price direction.

M1 (White) Has Been Declining and Is Now Flattening Out

Refer to Figure 7.7. Notice at the current point on the chart that:

1. The cycle is down with the MAs stacked down, indicating strong downward momentum.
2. M1 (white) has flattened out and gone horizontal.
3. The price tic has broken through M1 (white). Remember that when the MAs are stacked down, the lower BB and M1 (white) become support and resistance for the stock. Notice that the false Vs that have occurred since the MAs became stacked down.

We can now refer to our lower indicators to get an understanding of bias for the future price direction of the stock. When we assess our lower

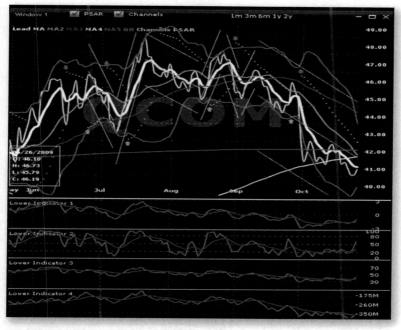

FIGURE 7.7   Chart of COM—M1 Declining

indicators, we see very strong indication of upward momentum. We see that L1, L2, and L3 have moved from the bottom of their scales and are now heading up. This is confirmation and validation that this next cycle will be up. We also see that L4 (red line) has crossed the blue line and the blue line is now headed up.

Every indicator is telling us that the stock price has upward bias. What we do not know is how much of an up cycle will occur before M1 rolls over again and cycles down.

In Chapter 9 we cover specific rules indicating when to utilize the tethered slingshot (TSS) and when to enter new positions. However, for now, the important concept to understand is that when M1 (white) flattens out, we look at our lower indicators to confirm and validate bias for the next cycle.

M1 (White) Has Been Rising and Is Now Flattening Out

Refer to the chart in Figure 7.8. Notice at the current point on the chart that:

1. The cycle is up with the MAs stacked up, indicating strong upward momentum.
2. M1 (white) has flattened out and gone horizontal.
3. The price tic has broken through M1 (white). Remember that when the MAs are stacked up, the upper BB and M1 (white) become support and resistance for the stock. Notice that the false Vs have appeared since the MAs stacked up.

FIGURE 7.8   Chart of CSCO—M1 Flattening

We can now refer to our lower indicators to get an understanding of bias for the future price direction of the stock. When we assess our lower indicators, we see very strong indication of downward momentum. We see that L1, L2, and L3 have moved from the top and are now heading down. We also see that L4 (red line) has crossed over the blue line from the top and is now pointing down.

Every indicator is telling us the stock price has downward bias. What we do not know is how much of a down cycle will occur before M1 rolls over again and cycles up.

You will see in Chapter 9 that we cover specific rules indicating when to TSS and when to enter new positions. However, for now, the important concept to understand is when M1 (white) flattens out, we look at our lower indicators to confirm and validate bias for the next cycle.

M1 (White) and M2 (Green) Have Converged and Are Moving Horizontally

As long as M1 and M2 are converged, do not trade. Wait for M1 to separate from M2 and turn either up or down.

Refer to Figure 7.9. Notice from the two convergence points on the chart that:

1. The cycle is confusing. The MAs are not stacked either way.
2. M1 (white) has flattened out and gone horizontal, and it is tracking M2 (green).

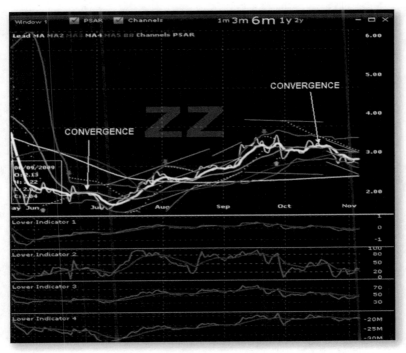

FIGURE 7.9 Chart of ZZ—M1 Convergence

When M1 and M2 converge, it is a signal to wait and have patience. This signal is also confirmed by the lower indicators because they are tracking horizontally or are in total disagreement. The stock is not cycling in either direction. The Vs being formed are too shallow to realize a return using a TSS. We are unsure of the cycle direction, so this is not an ideal new position. We must have patience with this stock for now. **These Advanced Charting indicators teach us patience, which remains an important part of the CSE covered call, LEAPS, and credit spread techniques.**

CHAPTER 8

The Second Chart: Window 2—Chart 2

You have now learned how to interpret the dramatic upward or downward movement of M1 (white). You also know when to look at the lower chart indicators for additional confirmation and validation of the V when M1 (white) flattens out. It is now time to discuss the second chart.

Window 2 – Chart 2 provides a visual indication of strength. It also shows signs of the four phases of a cycle. This helps us in confirming when to enter a new position, 10-cent rule, or trailing stop, and how long to remain in these trades. Chart 2 also helps to stay in a tethered slingshot (TSS) by showing us the strength and momentum of any downward movement during the momentum phase before the cycle enters into the exhaustion phase.

■ Modified Candlestick

For the second chart, we use a modified candlestick chart rather than a line chart. The main difference between a standard candlestick chart and the modified candlestick is the value used to create each bar or candle. Instead of using the open-high-low-close (OHLC) bars like in a standard candlestick, in the modified candlestick chart we use a modified version that smoothes the chart, making it very easy to read. Therefore, the modified candle shows the relative strength of a cycle and also notes key turning points in price action, reacting much like a moving average (MA).

Standard candlestick charts remove the visual noise of the charts, but they are complicated technical indicators that are extremely difficult to learn to use. Therefore, we have reformulated the standard candlestick chart to remove the noise and make it easier to use this important indicator.

Figures 8.1 and 8.2 are examples of two charts for LOW. Figure 8.1 is a standard candlestick chart, while Figure 8.2 is a modified candlestick chart.

FIGURE 8.1 Chart of LOW—Standard Candlesticks

Notice that the modified candlestick chart looks much smoother. In particular, it does not show the many false Vs that would occur on a line chart. Rather, the modified candlestick predominantly displays only key turning points in the stock. These key turning points are denoted by the candle changing from one color to another and also by the shortening of the candle body, which we discuss later in this chapter.

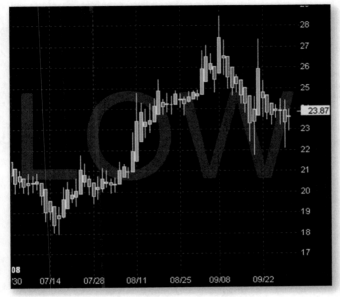

FIGURE 8.2   Chart of LOW—Modified Candlesticks

The simplicity of the modified candlestick chart should be evident. We have studied in detail what causes a cycle to move up, down, or turn flat. We have studied the lower indicators to show the correct timing to enter or exit a trade. The modified candlestick in Figure 8.2 simply shows when a cycle is about to be born. It shows when momentum begins and moves into exhaustion and finally when the cycle ends in the death phase. This is clearly visible in Figure 8.2 as the candle changes from red to green and the candle body length changes.

Understanding this indicator is very easy. All that is required is practice reviewing hundreds of charts to learn the unique characteristics of the modified candlestick as it cycles up and down and changes color from red to green and back to red.

▆ Understanding the Modified Candlestick

Now that we have established the modified candlestick as a valuable tool to give us a clear indication of momentum and turning points in price action, let's look a little deeper into exactly what the candles are telling us. We intentionally ignore technical details on the modified candlestick, such as how the candles are calculated and the individual names of candlestick patterns; knowing these details will not increase the ability to apply the modified candlestick technique.

Breaking Down Each Candle

Each point in the candle represents a piece of data. The chart in Figure 8.3 indicates the terms used to refer to each part of the candle (left) and what data various points on the candle are actually measuring (right).

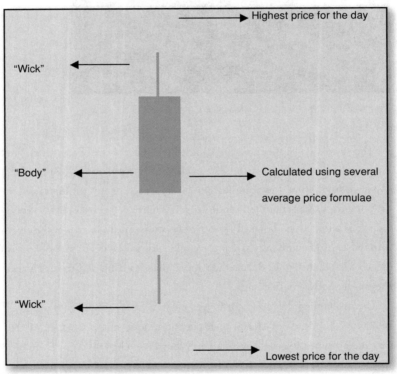

FIGURE 8.3   Parts of the Candle

The wick is the vertical line extension at the top and bottom of each candle. The body is the candle and is calculated using several average price formulas that are discussed in this book. When using the modified candlestick, the color (red or green) of the candle is not the only indicator; the size of the body and wicks relative to the previous day's candle are also indicators.

Using the Modified Candlestick to Understand Bias

Here we discuss and highlight precisely what indicators modified candlestick charts provide. As elsewhere, we break this analysis up into sections demonstrating upward bias, downward bias, and change in cycle.

At the end of this section, we integrate both Chart 1 and the modified candlestick Chart 2. Combining both charts in our analysis provides an extremely powerful picture of cycle direction, strength, and duration.

Upward bias in the stock price exists when:

1. The modified candlestick body is green. Green candles indicate upward momentum in the stock price.
2. The body of the candle is large or is expanding from the previous day.

Size is an important point to note. When the candle body remains large or is increasing in size from the previous day, this indicates strong upward momentum.

On the chart in Figure 8.4, note the increasingly large stepping-up candle bodies. **This indicates increasing upward momentum.**

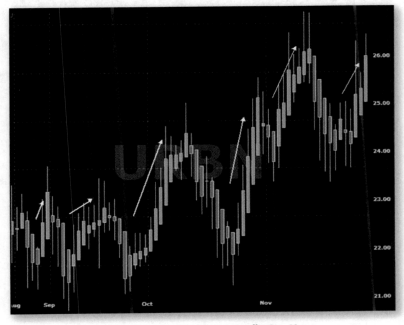

FIGURE 8.4   Chart of URBN—Modified Green Candles Bias Up

Downward bias in the stock price exists when . . .

1. The modified candlestick body is red. Red candles indicate downward momentum in the stock price.
2. The body of the candle is large or is expanding from the previous day.

Size is an important point to note. When the candle body remains large or is increasing in size from the previous day, this indicates strong downward momentum.

On the chart in Figure 8.5, note the increasingly larger candle bodies stepping down. **This indicates increasing downward momentum.**

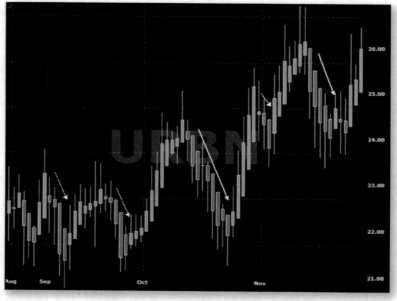

FIGURE 8.5   Chart of URBN—Modified Red Candles Bias Down

Cycle Exhausting/Potential Change in Trend

Another useful function of the modified candlestick gives a very good indication of a change in cycle direction. The changing of the length of the candle body is an early sign of the cycle entering into the exhaustion phase. The modified candlestick is a very helpful indicator in all aspects of the Compound Stock Earnings (CSE) covered call/LEAPS techniques including entering new positions and for assisting with TSS timing.

Changes from Upward Moving to Downward Moving

When the current upward movement in the stock price enters into the exhaustion phase, we see the changes on the modified candlestick shown in Figure 8.6:

1. The body length of the green candles starts to decrease in size.
2. The wick sizes of the green candles start to increase.
3. A red candle appears.

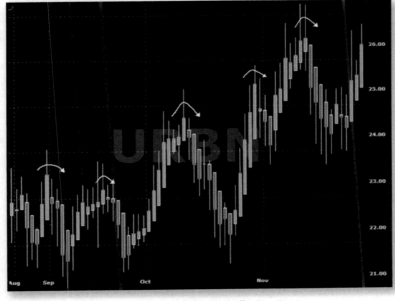

FIGURE 8.6 Chart of URBN—Modified Red Candles Bias Down

Changes from Downward Moving to Upward Moving

When the current downward movement in the stock price is beginning to exhaust, we see the changes on the modified candlestick shown in see Figure 8.7:

1. The body size of the red candles starts to decrease in length.
2. The wick sizes of the red candles start to increase.
3. A green candle appears.

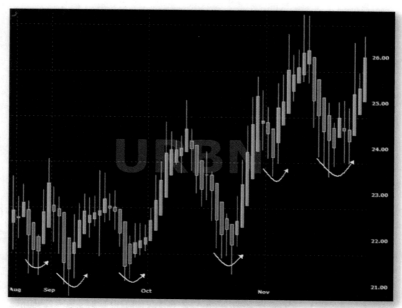

FIGURE 8.7 Chart of URBN—Modified Candlestick Bias Up

Adding the Moving Average Indicators to the Modified Candlestick Chart

Now that we understand the modified candlestick chart, it is time to add our moving average indicators. We use exactly the same moving averages as in the first chart (see Fig. 8.8). The combination of the modified candlesticks and these moving averages provides us with a powerful view of stock price direction and momentum and also smooths out the vast majority of false Vs. When looking at the modified candlestick, as shown in Figure 8.8, we use a three-month chart to see the detail.

From everything you have learned so far, you know that you can look at this chart and very clearly understand bias. To identify a change in price direction, you want to see M1 (white) flatten out with exhaustion. You want to see the price movement being confirmed by the modified candlestick bodies shortening and the wicks lengthening and eventually changing color. When these data are combined with the lower indicators, discussed in Chapter 7, you have a very clear view of future cycle and stock price direction.

The moving average indicators are necessary on Chart 2 for the modified candlesticks to calibrate the candle bodies. Do not use the moving

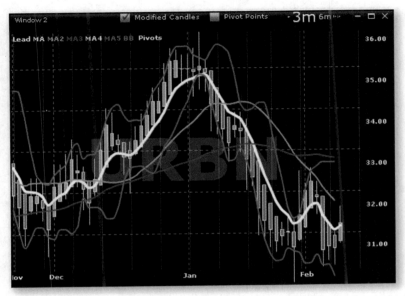

FIGURE 8.8 Chart of URBN—Modified Candle and Moving Averages

averages shown on Chart 2. Use only the moving average indicators shown in Chart 1.

Modified Candlestick Chart—Bollinger Band

One notable difference on Chart 2 is that we are using a shorter-period Bollinger band (BB). This shorter time setting will cause the Bollinger band to be more reactive and will show the BB pinch or squeeze discussed in Chapter 5. When the bands become pinched or squeezed, volatility is decreasing. This usually indicates a trend reversal. When you combine this information with the other indicators, you can decide when to enter new positions or TSSs.

The AA chart in Figure 8.9 shows another example of modified candles with all moving averages and the faster Bollinger bands.

Again, what is important to see here is M1 (white) flattening out and going horizontal, and the coinciding changes in the modified candlesticks (shortening of the bodies, increasing of the wicks, and changing color). These changes also coincide with a pinching of the Bollinger bands.

Detailed rules and chart examples of when to enter a new position, when to utilize a tethered slingshot (TSS), and when to buy to close (BTC) are presented in later in Chapter 9.

FIGURE 8.9 Chart of AA—Modified Candle and Bollinger Band

■ Pivot Points: Support and Resistance

Window 2 of Chart 2 (the right chart in Figure 8.10) shows the pivot point indicator turned on. This indicator has an on/off feature so we can turn pivot points on or off with either standard or modified candlesticks.

The pivot point is a technical indicator derived by calculating the numerical average of a stock's high, low, and closing prices. As a technical indicator, the pivot price is similar to resistance or support levels. If the price tic exceeds r1, a higher breakout is expected to occur. If the price tic exceeds r2, a higher breakout is expected to occur to the next point of resistance.

The same applies for support levels s1 and s2. If the price tic exceeds s1, a lower breakout is expected to occur. If the price tic exceeds s1, a lower breakout is expected to occur, and the tic may reach to the s2 level of support. As the price tic cycles up and down, it meets various levels of resistance and support. The pivot point serves as a predictive indicator showing different levels of where the price tic may cycle as it meets resistance and support.

Advanced charting provides 18 indicators to confirm and validate the possible direction of the price tic in either up or down cycles. By applying the information that the Bollinger bands and channels are showing on

Chart 1 with the pivot points on Chart 2, you can gain increased accuracy when entering or exiting a trade as the tic nears these levels of resistance and support.

Figure 8.10 (left) shows Window 1—Chart 1 channels, Bollinger bands with their price tic levels of resistance and support, and Window 2—Chart 2 (right) pivot points on levels of resistance and support.

FIGURE 8.10   Chart of LOW—Pivot Points

Charting is all about tracking cycle resistance and support. Therefore, advanced charting provides numerous indicators all searching for these data. The price tag shown on Chart 1 channel line (r1) and the price tag shown on Chart 2 pivot point (r1) may not be the same. Use the data shown as a guide to the general area of resistance and support. The same logic applies to r2 and s2 levels of resistance and support.

■ Lower Indicators: L5 to L8

As with the lower chart indicators on the line chart, the modified candlestick chart also has several lower chart indicators. Again, we use these lower chart indicators to get a better understanding of bias when lead MA M1 (white) goes flat.

The lower indicators on Chart 2 are very different from those on Chart 1. We use the modified candlesticks to identify key changes in price direction and momentum. Then we use Chart 2 lower indicators to confirm and validate that objective.

Lower Indicator 5—L5

Lower indicator L5 is another oscillator that provides an indication of overbought versus oversold. A signal line above 80 indicates an overbought condition. A signal line below 20 indicates an oversold condition. When interpreting this indicator, it is important to understand that a stock regularly continues to rise after lower indicator L5 has reached 80 and regularly continues to fall after it has reached 20. As such, when using L5, we are looking for the oscillator to move from overbought territory back below 80 and from oversold territory back above 20. Do not use L5 as an early indicator; use it just to validate the overbought versus oversold versus neutral position of stocks.

The chart in Figure 8.11 of WIRE is typical of what L5 will show relative to overbought versus oversold. Note the modified candlesticks and the position of L5 relative to its scale. Along with the modified candlestick, L5 does a fine job of smoothing out the Vs.

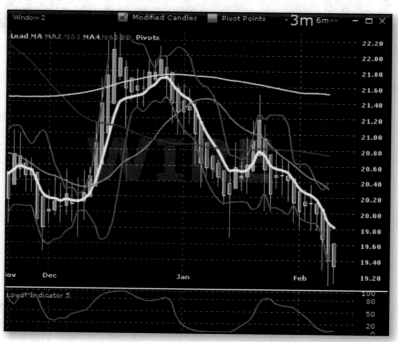

FIGURE 8.11   Chart of WIRE —L5

Lower Indicator 6—L6

Lower indicator L6 is another oscillator. It is smoothed to produce less, but much more accurate, signals. Like the modified candle, L6 removes the noise from the chart and helps smooth out the false Vs.

The chart of NDX in Figure 8.12 shows the L6 indicator. Notice the red line crossing the blue line and the relationship of these crossovers and the modified candles.

FIGURE 8.12 Chart of NDX—L6

It is important to watch where the red and blue lines are relative to the scale on the right. Where is the red line relative to the blue? Is the red above the blue line, or is it under the blue line? Is the red line moving away from the blue? L6 is an important indicator for timing entries into new positions and for TSSing.

Note that we do not trade with this indicator. When we use it in conjunction with all other indicators, our timing will improve.

Lower Indicator 7—L7

Lower indicator L7 in Figure 8.13 is another oscillator. It is smoothed to produce much more accurate signals than L6. Like the modified candlesticks and lower indicator L6, L7 removes the noise from the chart and helps smooth out the false Vs.

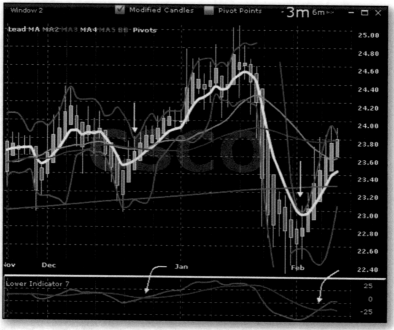

FIGURE 8.13   Chart of CSCO—L7

We interpret L7 in the same way as lower indicator L6. Where are the red and blue lines relative to the scale? Where is the red line relative to the blue signal line? Is the red line moving away toward the blue line? There is an obvious relationship between where L7 is relative to its scale and the high or low of the cycle on the chart. Notice the red line crossing the blue line in mid-December and the relationship of the crossovers to the red candles on the chart.

The lower indicators of advanced charting were designed and formulated to forecast the probabilities of cycle direction. Refer to the lower indicators when M1 turns flat, building your case to support your opinion of bias of the cycle and trend on Chart 1.

The momentum phase is the most important and most profitable phase of a cycle. This phase is also the most difficult to time for the perfect entry and exit.

L7 was formulated specifically to address this problem. L7 is a completely reformulated indicator that will show better than any indicator presented previously the perfect entry point of momentum after the L6 red to blue has crossed.

In Figure 8.13, we are watch L7 move from overbought territory at the top of its scale toward the oversold territory at the bottom of the scale. The crossover of the red line crossing the blue signal line is a critical event in applying the L7 indicator to our timing. As long as the blue signal line is pointed upward, momentum is still present, and we can remain in the trade. Exhaustion is not present. The same rule applies to the blue signal line pointed downward. It indicates that downward momentum is still present and we can remain in the TSS. Remember to watch both L6 and L7 closely as the red lines flatten out and turn back toward their blue signal lines.

We do not trade just with L7 but use it only in conjunction with all other indicators. Remember: You are looking for agreement, confirmation, and validation with the lower indicators. You are building your case to support your opinion of bias on Chart 1.

In Figure 8.14, note the first sign of a possible birth of a new cycle when the red line turns up from the bottom of the scale toward the blue signal line. Look for additional agreement and confirmation from other indicators that a new birth cycle is about to begin. L6 and L7 are formulated to track each other and also the modified candlesticks.

When the red line crosses the blue signal line at L6 (crossover 1) and is supported by other indicators agreeing that this is a new birth phase, enter the trade. You also can wait for more confirmation if the crossover is flat or enter the trade at L7 (crossover 2). Other indicators may indicate the probabilities that this will happen. In advanced charting, you must consider many subtleties.

This fact is important to understand: L6 tracks the modified candlesticks and detects the probability of the birth of a new cycle. Note the crossover of L6 and then soon after that the crossover of L7. A trade can be executed any time L6 red crosses blue and before red crosses blue on L7. If you place a trade after red has crossed blue on L7, you miss

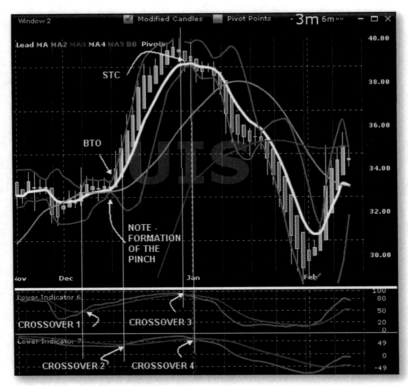

FIGURE 8.14 Chart of UIS—L6, L7

potential profits. The longer a trade is placed after L7 has crossed, it is possible the momentum phase is nearing the exhaustion phase.

When the red line turns flat or goes back toward the blue on L6 (crossover 3), this is the first sign of exhaustion.

In Figure 8.15, as M1 turns flat near the top of its cycle, the red line on L6 turns down toward the blue signal line (crossover 1). The cycle may have moved from the birth phase (crossover 2) to the momentum phase or onto the exhaustion phase (crossover 3). If this is confirmed as M1 continues to roll over, the next phase will be the death phase. The red line turning down and crossing the blue signal line on L7 confirms the death of one cycle and the birth of a new cycle (crossover 4).

Remember that we do not trade based on the data that we see with L6 and L7 but always refer back to our analysis of Chart 1 as to where the stock or index is relative to its current cycle. The lower indicators are used only to confirm when to enter or exit the trade.

FIGURE 8.15 Chart of UIS—L6, L7

Lower Indicator 8—L8

All lower indicators of advanced charting are designed and formulated to assist in confirming and validating our opinion of bias of the cycle and trend on Chart 1. **Identifying the birth phase of a cycle is paramount.**

As previously discussed, the momentum phase is the most profitable phase. Therefore, L8 is another indicator to help visualize the probabilities that a new birth cycle is about to begin. This, of course, may be followed by the momentum phase.

Refer to the chart in Figure 8.16. When using L8, we are watching the red and green colored bars move above and below the 0 line. The 0 line is M2. Prior to the beginning of a new birth phase, we are forewarned by the changing length of the bars as they get shorter toward the 0 line.

The crossing of the bars at the 0 line is the crossing of M1 to M2, either bias up or bias down. If the red and green bars remain above

FIGURE 8.16   Chart of BTU—L8

the 0 line, we know that the stock has been cycling up for weeks and perhaps months.

The same applies to the red or green bars. If they remain below the 0 line, we know the stock has been cycling down for weeks or perhaps months.

To identify a possible birth phase of a new up cycle, watch (refer to Figure 8.17, January) for the red bars as they extend to the lowest area relative to the L8 scale on the right. The red bars will continue to go lower. They may flatten out or a green bar may appear. This change from red to green is confirmation and validation that a new cycle may be about to start or has already started.

The new green bars get shorter in length as they move closer to the 0 line; this indicates that M1 is moving closer to M2. If the new cycle is true, the green bars continue to shorten until they cross the 0 line. After the crossover has occurred, a new set of green bars will continue to

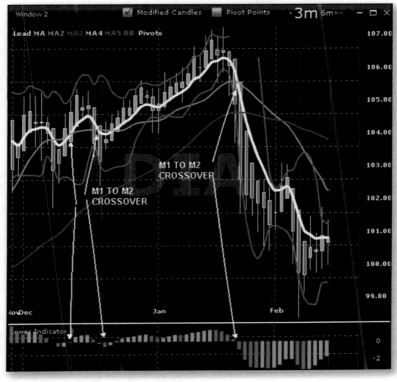

FIGURE 8.17 Chart of DIA—L8

extend above the 0 line. The green bars will continue to extend upward as long as the momentum phase is still valid.

When the upward momentum phase is about to change to exhaustion, the green bars begin to level off at the top of the scale. A red bar will appear followed by other shorter red bars. This may be a sign of a new birth phase as the red bars continue toward the 0 line.

We do not trade with L8 but use the data provided by the red/green bar graphic to visualize the probabilities of the birth of a new cycle.

Remember that advanced charting is designed to search for agreement, confirmation, and validation that a cycle is moving upward or downward. The 18 indicators that we have reviewed are all designed and formulated to search for that data. The indicators may agree or they may not agree. There are cases where there might be 100 percent agreement with the indicators. Therefore, different agreement/disagreement percentages increase risk and lower reward.

Recap of Advanced Charting

W e have covered a great deal of information in the previous eight chapters. In Chapter 9 we will recap the information and put all of the pieces together to enhance the level of understanding and ability to fully understand the Advanced Charting system.

1. The reformulated technical indicators of Advanced Charting search for answers to prove that the V is true or false, for both the regular V and the inverted V.
2. M1 tracks the movement of the Vs and will respond accordingly up, down, or flat.
3. M2 and M3 track the movement of M1 and respond accordingly, either going stacked up or stacked down. M1, M2, and M3 define the cycle—either up cycle or down cycle down
4. M4 defines the trend.
5. Extreme highs and lows of a cycle are defined by the upper Bollinger band (UBB) and the lower Bollinger band (LBB).
6. The PSAR alerts when a crossover has occurred on one or more of the lower indicators.
7. The channels are true points of resistance and support.
8. Zones are created as the tic moves between critical points of resistance and support.

9. The lower indicators for Chart 1 track the movement of the tic and M1. Each one searches numerous sources of data to confirm and validate the V.

10. The red or green modified candlestick clearly shows cycles as M1 moves from birth to death.

11. The Bollinger band pinch and flare are critical indicators to forewarn of a potential momentum move of the price tic.

12. The lower indicators for Chart 2 track the modified candles and Bollinger bands. L6 and L7 are critical to timing the entry and exit of trades.

By following the rules explained in this book, over time you will reach higher levels of mastery of this complicated subject. You will gain confidence in trading as your skill in interpreting the ebb and flow of M1 improves.

The charts in this chapter are examples of every critical phase as M1 cycles up and down, moving from birth, to momentum, to exhaustion, and then to death. Learn these phases well.

As M1 rolls through these cycles toward M2 touching, converging, and going stacked up or down, these important phases are forecasting the probabilities of where the tic will be in the near future or by expiration Friday (Friday target line, or FTL). Mastery of advanced charting enables you to recognize these critical points to enter and exit positions. This will mean fewer positions to manage, which equates to increased profits.

■ Entering New Positions on the Roll Up Above M2

Let's look at Figure 9.1. Reading Chart 1 on the left side we see that in November, M1 (white) has rolled over toward M2 (green). M1 (white) has briefly gone horizontal and has turned upward. M3 (blue) is still moving upward. This is a roll up occurring above M2. When a formation is stacked up and M1 rolls down toward M2, watch for a possible roll back up. **The more dramatically up M4 is, the greater probability of an early roll up.** You want to see the lower indicators on Chart 1 moving from the lower portion of their scales to the upper portion. You also want to see green candle bodies with increasing body length, and you want the lower indicators on Chart 2 to be moving upward. **Always review the lower indicators to evaluate how much upward momentum is present.**

FIGURE 9.1   Roll Up Above M2

■ Roll Up below M2

Refer to Figure 9.2. Reaching chart 1 in October and November, M1 (white) has dropped below the M2 (green). M1 (white) has gone horizontal and has turned up back toward M2. The formation is not stacked up when this occurs, but upward momentum is still strong. M1 can turn back up and cross back over M2. The formation would return to a stacked-up formation with strong upward momentum. You want to see the lower indicators low on their scales and turning up, which confirms and validates that the roll up may happen and could be strong. You want to see the candle bodies change from red to green.

FIGURE 9.2   Roll Up Below M2

■ Touch/Convergence: Example 1

Refer to Figure 9.3. When the moving averages (MAs) are stacked up (July) and M1 (white) rolls down and just touches M2 (green) and then turns back upward, generally this stock will continue an upward cycle if M4 is trending upward. When this happens, look at the lower indicators on Chart 1. They should all be in the oversold area and moving up. On Chart 2, you want today's candle bodies to be green. It is also ideal if the lower chart indicators are in the oversold position and are turning up. Upward momentum will be confirmed on subsequent days by increasing green body candles. Look at the L6 and L7 red-to-blue crossover. Are they low and ready to cross?

FIGURE 9.3   Touch/Convergence

■ Touch/Convergence: Example 2

Refer to Figure 9.4. If MAs are stacked up (September) and M1 (white) rolls over toward M2 and just touches M2 (green), watch for a roll.

FIGURE 9.4   Touch/Convergence

The touch may indicate continuation of the previous upward cycle. If M1 touches or stays converged on M2, this may be a sign of exhaustion. A horizontal or flattening M4 trend line increases the probability that this is happening. If a touch of M1 continues to convergence, wait. Many times when convergence is about to occur, the lower indicators are in disagreement. If M1 rolls upward after convergence, apply the rules of the roll up reviewed earlier.

■ True V/Double V

In Figure 9.5, we used the rule of the true V to consider entering a new position. If the single V does not yet confirm a new upward cycle, wait for a second V with a longer up tic leg to enter the position. The first V should be coming up off of the LBB very close to it. If the lower indicators confirm and validate the probabilities of a new upward cycle, the accuracy of the double V entering the position is extremely high. The lower indicators should be low relative to their scales with a lot of agreement.

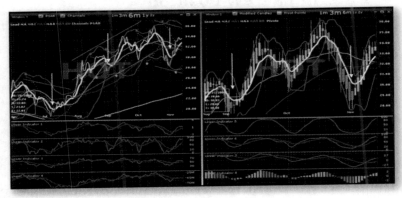

FIGURE 9.5   True V/Double V

■ The 10-Cent Rule

Identifying the False Regular and Inverted V

Earlier we touched on identifying the false V. Now is an ideal time to elaborate on this topic and how to use the false V to dramatically increase returns on new positions. By using technical indicators to establish positions where there is dramatic upward momentum (mid-July), very often you are in a position where the MAs are already stacked up or become stacked up after entry. As previously discussed, often when the MAs are stacked up, M1 (white) becomes support for the stock and the UBB becomes resistance. The stock will move sharply upward, channeling within these two indicators. When the charts show strong upward momentum, you may decide to let the stock run through the momentum phase (see Figure 9.6)

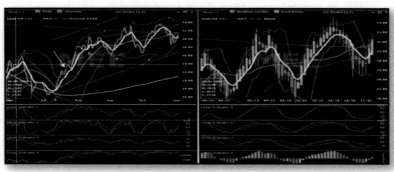

FIGURE 9.6 Chart of 10-Cent Rule, False V

■ Entering a New Position on the Roll Up

When M1 (white) has flattened out, gone horizontal, and turned up, many times the roll up is a perfect setup for entering a new position. Watch for higher highs and higher lows of M1 as it cycles up. If M1 begins to roll up again higher than the previous low, a new entry is possible. Confirm and validate with the lower indicators that the next cycle has room for momentum. You want to see a pinch and flare with a green candle on the modified candlestick chart. The lower indicators on Chart 2 should show upward bias. Refer to the L6 and L7 crossover rules (see Figure 9.7).

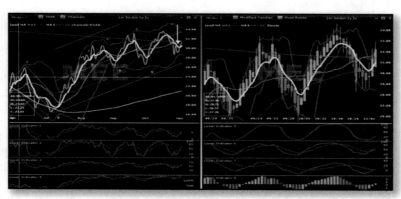

FIGURE 9.7 New Positions on the Roll Up

■ Upward Momentum Confirmed

Upward momentum is confirmed by long candle bodies. On Chart 1 in Figure 9.8, the price tic of the stock is hugging the UBB. The MAs are beginning to stack up. M1 (white) becomes support. At this point you have already BTC the call under the 10-cent rule and are now long the LEAPS. Do not place a trailing stop on the stock or LEAPS. Rather, hold the position and wait for the technicals to tell you when to exit.

FIGURE 9.8   Momentum Confirmed

■ Exit the Position When Price Tic Falls Through M1

You are now holding a position with the potential for extremely large gains. Most often M1 will become support and UBB will become resistance for the stock, and the stock will move in that channel. You should be monitoring L6 and L7, watching the red line as it turns flat and down toward the blue signal line. Immediately exit the position (sell the stock or LEAPS) when the price tic crosses below M1 on Chart 1 and when the red line crosses the blue signal line on L6. Refer to the crossover rules of L6 and L7 on Figure 9.9.

■ TSS for Income

The tethered slingshot (TSS) for income is a key technique that allows the continued generation of income on positions that have declined in value or positions investors wish to hold for generating income. In this section, we highlight how to use these advanced technical indicators to

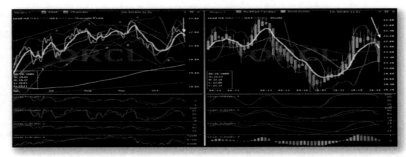

FIGURE 9.9 Exit the Position

improve efficiency with the TSS technique. Efficiency increases will be
noticed in these areas:

- Improved timing on when to sell a TSS.

- Improved timing on when to buy back a TSS.

- Improved timing on when not to sell a TSS.

  We TSS when:

- The timing to enter a TSS is agreement and validation with all of the
  indicators that the current cycle may be changing from an upward to
  a downward cycle.

- The change of a cycle may occur and is expected anytime regardless if
  the cycle is stacked up or not.

- A possible roll (down) of M1 occurs toward M2 with various degrees
  of agreement of the lower indicators.

- We watch for the crossovers of L6 and L7 with both indicators high
  relative to their scales.

■ TSS: Stacked Up with M1 Rolling Down

In Figure 9.10, the price tic in mid-October on Chart 1 shows an inverted
V and has crossed M1. M1 has rolled over and is now pointing down.
The lower indicators are high relative to their scales with the red lines
either crossed over the blue line or about to cross it. There is agreement
and validation that the birth of a down cycle is about to start. You can see

several TSS opportunities mid-October, mid-November, and another one the end of December. Refer back to the instructions for L6 and L7 and how the crossings of the red lines to the blue signal line indicate a TSS entry. If Chart 1 was stacked up with a dramatic M4 trend line, caution should be applied and a possible roll up may occur. This move is confirmed and validated if M1 continues to turn down. Analyze the previous highs and lows of M1 on Chart 1 to determine the probable depth of the next low cycle of M1.

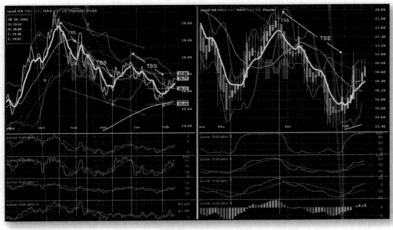

FIGURE 9.10 Chart of TSS—Stacked Up with M1 Rolling Down

■ TSS: Upward Moving M1 and Roll at M2

In Figure 9.11, the price tic shows a V in mid-October. M1 rolls over and turns toward M2. The tic is at the UBB and now headed down. The lower indicators of Chart 1 are all high relative to their scales. The UBB and LBB are wide apart, and the probabilities are high for a good down cycle. Watch for a possible roll up of M1 but anticipate a deep down cycle.

The price tic shows a V. M1 (white) rolls over at M2 (green) and turns down under M2 (green). The modified candlesticks turn from green to red, indicating downward momentum. The lower indicators are showing downward bias. Note the red line crossing the blue line on L6 and L7.

FIGURE 9.11 Chart of TSS—Upward Moving M1 and Roll at M2

■ When to Buy Back a TSS

In this section, we discuss the ideal timing to buy to close (BTC) TSS. By using our advanced technical indicators, you can easily identify the false V and validate the true V. Doing this allows you to stay in a TSS longer, resulting in larger buyback returns.

A BTC is executed when signs of exhaustion begin to show in the down cycle. Signs of exhaustion include:

1. M1 (white) begins to turn flat or roll up.
2. The lower indicators are setting up in the lower areas of their scales.
3. Red candles on Chart 2 begin to shorten in length.
4. The red line on L6 begins to turn up toward the blue line.
5. A green bar shows on L8.

This is when to buy to close a TSS with signs of cycle exhaustion.

TSS: Upward-Moving M1 and Roll at M2

The trigger to BTC the TSS is when the price tic crosses through M1 (white). Note the red-to-blue crossover of L6 in Figure 9.12. This will also coincide with the modified candlestick showing upward bias (red candle bodies getting smaller with larger wicks or a green candle appearing).

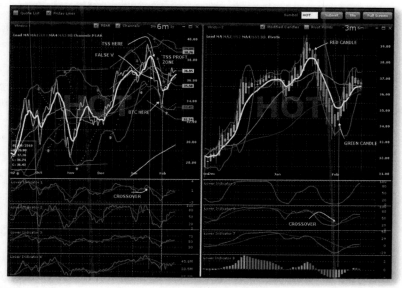

FIGURE 9.12 Chart of TSS—Upward-Moving M1 and Roll at M2

CHAPTER 10

RS: Advanced Charting Relative Strength Indicator

The relative strength (RS) indicator was presented at the 2010 Compound Stock Earnings Masters Seminar, It was tested and back-tested for months with hundreds of stocks prior to that presentation.

Earlier in this book, we reviewed and discussed four phases of a cycle: birth, momentum, exhaustion, and death. Understanding these four phases and correct chart interpretation increases the probability of correct entry and exits of trades.

Advanced Charting is continually searching and testing indicators to improve its accuracy. The strength or weakness of a stock relative to the overall market is an important indicator of market direction and momentum.

If the indices are moving lower or down, but the stock you are interested in trading is holding steady or moving up, ask yourself: Does this stock have strength? If indices are moving higher or up, but the stock you are interested in trading is holding steady or moving downward, ask yourself: Does this stock have weakness?

The movement of the indices up or down with your stock moving against that direction or in the opposite direction is valuable data to apply to your trading.

Relative strength compares one thing to something else. RS is dependent on something else for significance. It is a measurement of a price cycle that indicates how a stock is performing relative to other stocks in its industry. The calculation divides a stock's price performance by the price performance of an appropriate index for the same time period. With the exception of RUT, the Russell 2000 Index, all indices mirror each other as they cycle up and down. Advanced charting RS uses one index as its comparison index, but the index may change according to market conditions.

Advanced Charting relative strength uses a new methodology of its application as opposed to that previously found in earlier versions of Advanced Charting in order to identifying strength and momentum. RS combined with the advanced charting indicators provides an extremely powerful method of seeing the strength or weakness of any stock.

The momentum phase is an extremely important phase in the life cycle of a stock. This phase is where most profit is realized with the highest returns possible. Let's review momentum with relative strength.

What Is Momentum?

- Momentum is the measurement of the speed or velocity of price changes and the rate of the rise or fall in stock price.

- Momentum is a very useful indicator of strength or weakness.

- Charting history has shown that momentum is far more useful during rising markets than during falling markets.

- Markets rise more often than they fall.

- Usually bull markets last longer than bear markets.

Relative Strength

- The RS indicator is a very easy indictor to understand. The visual characteristics of this indicator are very simple.

- Advanced charting uses one or more indices as its comparison index of relative strength.

- The RS indicator can be applied to the interpretation of strength or weakness with upward-, flat, and downward-cycling stocks.

■ Comparing the Relative Strengths

Here we look at the different relative strengths and compare each type.

Relative Strength: AAP—Upward-Cycling M1

See Figure 10.1.

- Note that in mid-May, the RS red line drops, but M1 and the price tic remain flat. **This is relative strength.**

- Note how M1 and the price tic move upward as RS continues to drop lower.

- This stock continues to show strength against a weak and downward-moving RS. This is relative strength.

- The RS indicator is used only with Window 1–Chart 1.

FIGURE 10.1 Chart 1 AAP—Upward-Cycling M1

The AAP chart example clearly shows relative strength as the RS red line drops lower and M1 and the price tic move higher. This indicates strength against a falling index.

· If pre-market is a green or an up market day, the probabilities are very high that this stock will explode into momentum because of the relative strength it has held for weeks and months. It will respond like a loaded spring waiting to be released.

Relative Strength: SA—Horizontal-Moving M1

See Figure 10.2 Note that in July, the RS red line moves horizontally as M1 and the price tic move downward. **This is relative weakness.**

■ Note in September how M1 and the price tic move horizontally mirroring RS. **This is relative strength.**

Relative strength is very obvious on the chart of AAP. RS can also be used with stocks that have a flat or horizontal-moving M1.

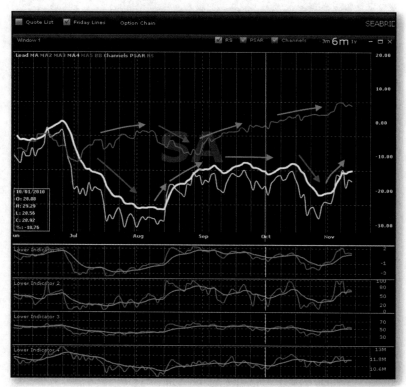

FIGURE 10.2   Chart 2 SA—Horizontal-Moving M1

You can see from the chart in Figure 10.2 how the red RS indicator moves horizontally and M1 and the price tic also move horizontally, mirroring the direction of the cycles. Even though there isn't a lot of upward momentum present, small upward momentum cycles, as seen in mid-August and the end of October, still are obvious and can be traded by more aggressive and experienced traders.

Relative Strength: SA—Downward-Moving M1

See Figure 10.3.

- Note that in July, the RS red line moves horizontally as M1 and the price tic move downward. **This is relative weakness.**

Relative weakness is very obvious on the chart of LHB. Note that M1 and the price tic are moving downward and spreading away from the red

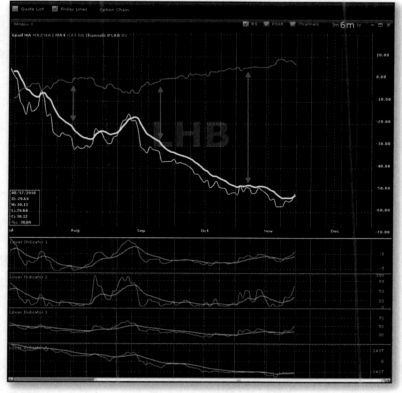

FIGURE 10.3 Relative Strength: SA—Downward-Moving M1

RS indicator. This is relative weakness. For covered calls, LEAPS or momentum trades, relative weakness stocks should be avoided because repeating downward cycles are evident and probably will continue.

■ Conclusion

Mastery of these advanced technical analysis tools, as with any new technique, may take several months of implementation during live trading.

Once you have gained confidence in these indicators, you will be able to trust what the charts are telling you and act accordingly. Once you gain trust in these indicators, you will stop second-guessing your trading decisions and will trade with confidence and greater precision.

In time, you will no longer look at these indicators separately but together, and they will immediately give you a very clear indication of probable future price direction.

Attend many seminars. Each time you do, you will be exposed to more charting subtleties, which will improve your mastery of advanced charting.

It's all in the charts.

CHAPTER 11

Momentum Trading and Trading the Moment

If you have attended the Advanced Charting seminar and have studied this manual, you are now familiar with the methodologies of this powerful charting system. Thousands of closed trades by Advanced Charting graduates are proof of the accuracy of this charting method. If you want to validate this, go to www.compoundstockearnings.com/wantproof.

Regardless of what Compound Stock Earnings (CSE) technique a client chooses to trade—be it covered calls, LEAPS, credit spreads, SSHs, momentum trades, or trading the moment—Advanced Charting increases the returns of the technique due to the greater accuracy of chart interpretation to time the entry and exit of positions.

CSE has raised the bar again with the introduction of Advanced Charting streaming data charts. Imagine having a streaming data charting system where pricing data for stocks, exchange-traded funds (ETFs), and indexes are streaming into the charting system in real time. What does that mean? That means you can watch the price tick move up and down according to the heartbeat of the market and the heartbeat of every stock, ETF, or index. Imagine watching volatility strengthen and weaken according to the marketplace. The methodologies of chart interpretation are the same as in Advanced Charting, but now it is streaming, so a trader can watch the indicators moving up and down to enter and exit trades.

In fact, according to client surveys, the application of Advanced Charting streaming data charts has resulted in closed daily trades or day trades of 3 percent per day with home-run trades of 50 percent or more. This is possible only with the application of Advanced Charting streaming data charts.

The Advanced Charting methodologies, and mastering the multitude of subtleties, is the game changer and the reason for these consistently high day-trade returns.

■ Momentum Trades

First, before we study streaming data charts, let's review the evolution of Advanced Charting momentum trading to Advanced Charting streaming data charts.

You may recall the review of four important phases as M1 cycles up and down: the birth phase, momentum phase, exhaustion phase, and death phase. All stocks, ETFs, and indexes will cycle up and down in these four phases.

The birth phase identifies a potential sweet spot where the indicators on the chart and the lower indicators confirm, validate, and agree that the probabilities are very high that the next cycle will move upward over the short term.

It is through the correct chart interpretation of an upward-trending M4 trend line and a sweet spot that the Advanced Charting momentum call (MC) trade evolved. The MC trade is a trade where the trader purchases a long far out option month. The M4 trend line and sweet spot trade entry increase the probabilities of upward momentum to last for several days or weeks. Those familiar with option trading will immediately realize the potential profit possibilities through leverage, buying an inexpensive call option, a tight bid/ask spread, and the correct chart entry of the trade.

It is only with Advanced Charting that a trader can see the birth phase to enter the momentum phase of the price cycle of the stock, ETF, or index. Applying this simple methodology creates consistent winning trades, one trade after another.

Refer to chart 86 of COO in Figure 11.1. Notice the upward-trending M4 trend line. This trend line is a powerful predictor of future birth phases, repeating one after another over the life cycle of this stock.

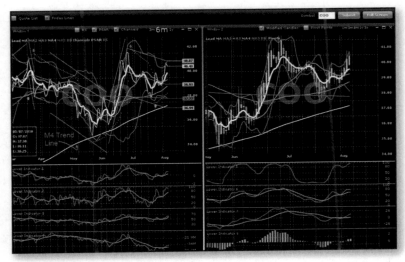

FIGURE 11.1 Chart 86 of COO—M4 Trend Line

Next, chart 87 of COO (Figure 11.2) identifies confirmation, validation, and agreement with the lower indicators that the next cycle for this stock is at a sweet spot. Notice where M1 cycles down and begins to turn flat. Notice the lower indicators L1 through L8 and how they agree with each other.

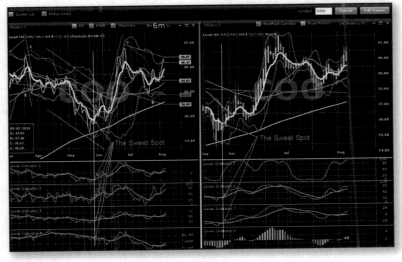

FIGURE 11.2 Chart 87 of COO—Sweet Spot

Imagine a trading service where hundreds of Advanced Charting graduates trained to identify upward-trending M4 trend lines and potential sweet spots submit their stocks, ETFs, or indexes to a common database. This database is called an Advanced Charting Platinum Selections Watch List.

This list may have up to 70 to 80 stocks about to move into the birth phase sweet spot. Successful, profitable trading is first knowing what to trade. Knowing what to trade and using Advanced Charting methodologies create a winning combination to remove the guesswork and emotions from trading. If you want more information about the Advanced Charting Platinum Selections service, contact the CSE office at www.compoundstockearnings.com.

■ Tomato Fields

To best illustrate knowing what to trade to be a profitable trader, refer to the photo of a tomato field shown in Figure 11.3.

FIGURE 11.3   Tomato Field

The healthy tomato plant is a perfect example of a good company with an upward-trending M4 trend line. A healthy tomato plant will produce multiple good tomatoes over the life of the plant. Assume you are a tomato farmer and you had to harvest this tomato field alone. How long would it take you to harvest the best tomatoes?

What if you had hundreds or thousands of other trained tomato farmers walking this field and numerous other fields in search of the best tomatoes to harvest? This is the Advanced Charting Platinum Selections Watch List: a harvest of many healthy tomato plants about to produce one sweet spot after another.

The harvest will provide an abundance of stocks to trade every day with an overflowing inventory of momentum trades just waiting for you to trade (see Figure 11.4). Hundreds of tomatoes are farmed and screened for quality control.

FIGURE 11.4 Tomato Harvest

Consider the facts: hundreds or thousands of trained Advanced Charting chartists submitting stocks about to move into the birth phase. You select what to trade based on the sweet spot forming on the charts and enter the trade. You exit the trade at the first signs of the exhaustion phase. This is a momentum trade.

■ Recap of the Momentum Trade

Momentum of the price cycle is evident when the proprietary indicators of Advanced Charting all align to produce the high probability of a sweet spot. This development leads to the creation of momentum trading. In a momentum trade, in order to take advantage of the high probabilities of explosive upside movement in the stock price, a LEAPS or a short-term option is purchased without the simultaneous sale of the short call.

The result is a position with a very high likelihood of significant short-term profits as the stock moves from the birth phase into the momentum phase. With the accuracy of Advanced Charting, we can consistently identify the birth of a new cycle and buy the long option without selling the short call. Conversely, the momentum trading put is buying the long put option based on the put sweet spot on the charts to take advantage of explosive downward movements in the stock price. Again, the consistent profitability of these trading methods is possible only due to the accuracy of Advanced Charting.

■ Trading the Moment

First, there was the development of Advanced Charting with the 20 re-formulated and redefined technical indicators and a new methodology of chart interpretation. Further improvements evolved to the momentum trade, which is a LEAPS trade on steroids.

With the perfection of Advanced Charting and hundreds of back-tested trades, the trading the moment (TTM) day trade with streaming data charts has become the most profitable trading method of all CSE techniques.

For the trader who wants excitement and wants to know within seconds and minutes whether a trade will be profitable. The TTM is a game changer for sure.

Earlier, we reviewed a brief explanation of the TTM. Now the TTM deserves a more detailed analysis, because it is a life-changing method of trading.

It is a fact in the world of trading that day trading options can be a very profitable method of trading. In fact, it is the most profitable of all methods of option trading. It can also be very risky, as noted in the pages of boilerplate on all brokers' websites. Why? Most day traders attempt to capture profits by assuming the direction of the price tick of a stock either by trading a call option or by trading a put option—hoping to be on the correct side of the cycle.

Advanced Charting streaming data charts changed the "I hope I am right" to "I know I am right" with a high degree of probability that I am on the correct side of the cycle when I enter that trade.

The TTM technique is a day trade where the position is entered and exited for a profit on the same day. These TTM positions are typically opened and then closed for a profit within seconds, minutes, or hours. TTM trades can produce 3 percent returns or more per day. Some TTM traders are averaging 7 percent to 10 percent or more per day. Yes, you read this correctly. Can you imagine in 2008 when Advanced Charting was first introduced that just a few years later CSE clients would be day trading and making returns in one day that were in the past made in an entire month? This is possible only because of Advanced Charting methodologies, logic of chart interpretation, and trading rules.

It is simply a fact that if you learn the CSE methodology, you can be one of the rare traders who consistently profit in the option market. You, too, can generate these 3 percent or more returns per day on a consistent basis if you are correctly educated and disciplined. The CSE education will change your life as it has for thousands of our clients all over the world.

What Are Streaming Data Charts?

Advanced Charting streaming data charts will allow the trader to track up to three different stocks, ETFs, or indexes at a time. The slide shown in Figure 11.5 has three stocks, AAPL, ALK, and ED. By tracking three stocks, the trader is watching for volatility of up and down cycles with the objective to select one with the most volatility to day trade.

Notice that the graphics of these three charts are similar to the Advanced Charting charts illustrated throughout this book, but more specifically chart 86 of COO. In Figure 11.5, notice the charts and their lower indicators. The same chart interpretation and methodology applied to Advanced Charting are applied the same way with streaming data charts.

The Advanced Charting methodology is confirming, validating, and looking for agreement with the indicators that a sweet spot is forming for either a call or put option trade. The difference, however, is obvious because the data are streaming and live as you watch the price tick, M1, and all of the indicators move as new, fresh data stream into the charts.

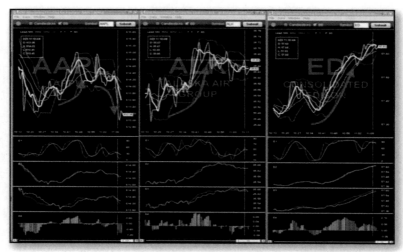

FIGURE 11.5   Chart 88 of AAPL, ALK, ED

You will see up and down cycles form in beautiful harmony as you prepare to enter your trade.

There is a saying that a picture is worth a thousand words. The next two charts, Figure 11.6a, chart 89 of TLT, and Figure 11.6b, chart 90 of AAPL, say it all. Notice the TLT chart showing a strong upward cycle. This would obviously be a very good call trade. Notice the AAPL chart showing a strong downward cycle. This shows a very strong put trade.

Detailed Explanation of Chart 89 of TLT— Upward Cycle

1. M1 has cycled down and is about to turn up from a birth phase.
2. E1 lower indicator is low relative to its scale with the red line crossing through the blue line.
3. E2 lower indicator is low relative to its scale with red and blue lines turned up.
4. E3 lower indicator is low and red and about to cross up through the blue line.
5. E4 lower indicator shows green bars getting shorter and about to cross over the 0 line.
5c. This is the support target of the previous down cycle. M1 turns up from its birth phase and heads upward toward 5b.

5b. This is the 50 percent target area, which begins to confirm that upward momentum has started.

5a. This is the resistance target of the previous down cycle. M1 has crossed
through the 50 percent target and crossed through the resistance target at 5a. It confirms and validates that upward momentum is present.

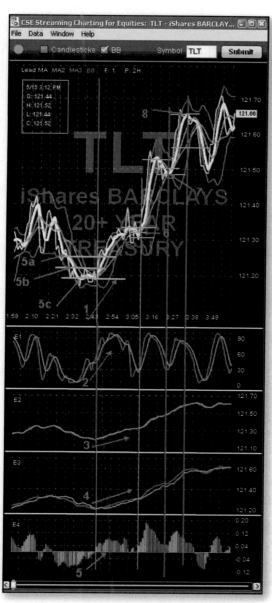

FIGURE 11.6a   Chart 89 of TLT

6. M1 rolls over and down, and the same chart analysis of the cycle is applied with support, 50 percent target, and a resistance point like the analysis at 5c, 5b, and 5a.
7. M1 rolls over and down again, and the same analysis of the cycle is applied with support, 50 percent target, and a resistance target.

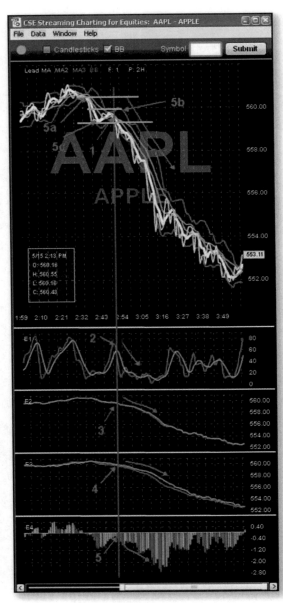

FIGURE 11.6b   Chart 90 of AAPL

8. M1 rolls over and down again, but now caution must be realized because E2 and E3 are high relative to their scales and the exhaustion phase may be starting.

A trader's goal is to always protect profit made in all trades, so closing out this call trade is the wise choice. As you align your eyes to the vertical red line, you can see that confirmation, validation, and agreement are present with all of the indicators. This increases the probability that this call trade would be profitable.

Detailed Explanation of Chart 90 of AAPL—Downward Cycle

5a. M1 rolls over and turns down. M1 continues down, and turns flat at 5c. E2 and E3 are high relative to their scales, which indicates that a new down cycle is about to begin. M1 turns up from 5c. You monitor M1 to see if it breaks through its 50 percent target. It does not, but instead turns over and begins to cycle down under its 50 percent target.
1. M1 turns over and begins to cycle down.
2. E2 is high with the red line turned down and about to cross the blue line.
3. E3 is high relative to its scale and already turned down with both the red and blue lines turning down.
4. E4 is high relative to its scale and has already turned down with the red line under the blue.
5. Both red and green bars are under the 0 line, and red bars are appearing.

M1 breaches the 5c support line with confirmation, validation, and agreement with the lower indicators. The probabilities are very high that this would be a very good put trade. Align your eyes to the vertical red line. The streaming data charts are unfolding before your eyes for another put trade. And this occurs over and over with the real-time data feed. The charts are alive and cycling up and down until the market closes. Then—a new day and it starts all over.

The 1-5-15 Chart Setup

After you decide what stock, ETF, or index to trade, you can set the streaming charts to the 1-5-15 setup. This setup allows you to focus on one trade at a time to monitor the exact point to enter a trade and the bias of the short-term trend with the 5 and 15 charts.

The chart on the far left in Figure 11.7 will default to frequency 1 minute, as will all charts that you open. The middle chart is set at frequency 5 minutes, and the third chart is set at frequency 15 minutes. The 5 and 15 charts are lagging behind the frequency 1 chart, and this exposes the overall bias of the short-term trend. Remember, with streaming charts you are day trading, so the trend is short and not long as it is with Advanced Charting.

FIGURE 11.7 Chart 91 of GOOG Set at 1-5-15

Detailed Explanation of the 1-5-15 Chart Setup

1. This point identifies where M1 has turned flat. This is the resistance point of the next down cycle as M1 cycles down to point #2 and then to point #3.

2. This point is marked after M1 starts to turn flat again at point #3, which identifies the next birth phase. Point #2 is the approximate 50 percent target of the previous down cycle. The previous down cycle is from point #1 to point #3.

3. M1 has turned flat and is just starting to turn up as a new birth phase. The marking of the resistance, support, and 50 percent target line is called the retracement rule. You will use this rule to monitor strength and weakness of the new birth phase cycle. As M1 turns upward, will it breach the 50 percent target or roll

under it? Will M1 breach the 50 percent target and move on to the resistance point? You will monitor M1 as it moves upward toward these targets. As this unfolds, you review the lower indicators for confirmation, validation, and agreement (CVA). Notice the vertical red line and align the lower indicators to see how much CVA is present.

4. As M1 moved upward from the birth phase into momentum, it is obvious that bias is up and becoming stronger. The upward cycle is now stacked up. (Remember this term from Advanced Charting?) This CVA is clear to enter a call trade because the direction of bias is obvious.

5. Notice the red vertical lines that mark every point where the price tick has gone above, below, or close to the upper (UBB) or lower (LBB) Bollinger bands. We know from Advanced Charting that when the price tick breaches or gets close to either band, it will reverse its path and head toward the opposite band. But what you must be aware of is overall bias of the short-term trend. Just because the tick is above the UBB, this does not guarantee that the tick will not stop and reverse well above the LBB and head back toward the UBB. Notice the tick reversing its path and heading back up to the UBB during the strong upward cycle at #4.

6. Point #6 marks the price tick as it breaches the UBB. You know the tick will come back inside the UBB and may head toward the LBB. You look at the lower indicators to determine the probabilities that the tick will cycle down. Notice CVA. How much CVA is there that a new down cycle is about to occur? Notice the tick as it Vs down to the LBB and Vs back and forth as the lower indicators are high relative to their scales as all indicators begin to move down.

Short-Term Trend

The upward short-term trend is also confirmed by the 5 and 15 charts. Notice the white circled time marks at approximately 2:34 p.m. on all three charts. Notice the CVA showing bias up. Also notice when M1 started to turn flat and roll over at point #6 on chart 1, there is less CVA of upward bias. There are now indications that the short-term trend is changing from upward bias to downward bias. Experienced TTM traders may enter quick short call and put trades during this transition phase, but for new TTM traders it is best to wait for a sweeter sweet spot.

Look at the far right of all three charts. Chart 1 shows downward bias of this cycle. Chart 2 is not stacked up or stacked down, and the lower indicators are CVA that bias is down. Chart 3 also shows bias is now down with CVA with the lower indicators. Remember, do not expect to see 100 percent CVA; you are looking for the most CVA that is present on all three charts.

All decisions on when to pull the trigger to enter a call or put trade are made from chart 1. You enter a call trade only when E1 is low relative to its scale with CVA. You enter a put trade when E1 is high relative to its scale.

The 1-5-15 chart setup changes the functionality of the lower indicators on the 5 and 15 charts. E1 on the 5 chart functions more like L1 in Advanced Charting. Go back and review the details of the L1 indicator in Advanced Charting. The E2 and E3 indicators on the 5 chart change to function like L6 and L7 in Advanced Charting.

The 15 chart is showing longer-term trend bias. If bias is up on both the 5 and 15 charts on a market up or green day, you know you should be able to trade numerous call trades. The opposite applies if bias is down on the 5 and 15 charts on a market down or red day; then you know you will be able to trade numerous put trades.

Remember: if you do not see CVA, do not trade TTMs until you improve your trading skills and charting knowledge. Many times a best trade is *no* trade. There will always be a new trading day with new charts with new sweet spots.

Edwin L. Watanabe owned a commercial design business for almost thirty years. He traded as a hobby and, like many traders, tried to figure out how technical indicators really worked. It was through frustration that he created his own charting method. After years of testing and back-testing he reformulated how the indicators worked so they would either agree or disagree as to the direction of the next cycle. He re-defined how to interpret the indicators and created a new rule-based methodology in their application. He is the charting specialist and charting consultant for Compound Stock Earnings. He is a trader, Advanced Charting seminar instructor and also oversees the Advanced Charting Platinum Selection services which include—Momentum Trading, Trading The Moment™ and Forex Currency Trading. He proved that with the right charting tool, you can literally trade anything, and he coined the phrase: It's all in the charts™.

A ll readers of *Advanced Charting* are entitled to a month of free access to our Advanced Charting program. This program includes:

1. Access to the Advanced Charting tool discussed in this book.
2. Access to our Advanced Charting Platinum Selections service.

This service provides daily stock selections based on the proprietary criteria of Advanced Charting. Additionally, a two-hour interactive webinar is conducted each week to provide new clients with regular coaching on the application of the Advanced Charting technique. The daily position selections and weekly coaching webinars combine to make Advanced Charting Platinum Selections the highest-returning and most unique stock selection service on the planet.

Sign up for a 30-day free trial at: www.compoundstockearnings.com/ freeACPSbook and see how hundreds of our clients are using Advanced Charting Platinum Selections to generate returns of up to 3 percent per day.

lower indicators and
direction of, 98
moving averages and
direction of, 18–19
phases of, 15–18, 33, 43, 85
review of, 49
supplementary MAs and,
44–45
support and resistance
points, 57
trend lines and, 13, 14
understanding, 3
upward, 15–16

D

Day trading
streaming data charting
system and, 129–136
trading the moment (TTM),
128–129
Death phase, 49
of downward-cycle, 17
modified candlestick chart
and, 87
of upward-cycle, 16
DELL chart M1, M2, M3
stacked up, 31
Delta low bridge (DLB), 3
DIA chart, 13, 14
Divergence, 79

E

Exhaustion phase, 49
of downward-cycle, 16–17

lower indicators of, 103
modified candlestick chart
and, 87, 90–92
signs of, 114
of upward-cycle, 15–16

F

False V, 53, 55, 56
Flare, 53, 67–68, 110
Friday target line (FTL),
61–62, 106

H

"Hippo" technical indicator, 53

I

Index movement, relative
strength and, 117–118

L

Lead dog, 19, 71
LEAPS, 1, 48
channel indicators and, 57
modified candlestick charts
and, 90
moving averages and, 71
patience and, 84
relative weakness stocks
and, 122
Lower Bollinger bands (LBB),
52, 61, 135
Lower indicator 1, 74–75
Lower indicator 2, 75–77
Lower indicator 3, 77–78

M